POLITICS and the COURTS

POLITICS *and the* COURTS

Toward a General Theory of Public Law

BARBARA M. YARNOLD

New York
Westport, Connecticut
London

Copyright Acknowledgments

The author and publisher gratefully acknowledge permission to reprint portions of the following copyrighted materials.

Yarnold, Barbara M. 1990. "Federal Court Outcomes in Asylum-Related Appeals 1980–1987: A Highly 'Politicized' Process." *Policy Sciences* 23(4) (November): 291–306. Copyright © 1990 by Kluwer Academic Publishers. Reprinted by permission of Kluwer Academic Publishers.

Yarnold, Barbara M. 1991. *International Fugitives: A New Role for the International Court of Justice*. New York: Praeger. Copyright © 1991 by Barbara M. Yarnold. Reprinted with permission.

Yarnold, Barbara M., ed. 1991. *The Role of Religious Organizations in Social Movements*. New York: Praeger. Copyright © 1991 by Barbara M. Yarnold. Reprinted with permission.

Library of Congress Cataloging-in-Publication Data

Yarnold, Barbara M., 1961–
    Politics and the courts : toward a general theory of public law /
    Barbara M. Yarnold.
        p.   cm.
    Includes bibliographical references (p.   ) and index.
    ISBN 0-275-94166-3 (alk. paper)
    1. Political questions and judicial power—United States.
    2. Judicial process—United States.   3. Courts—United States.
    4. Public law—United States.   5. Law and politics.   I. Title.
    KF8700.Y37   1992
    342.73—dc20
    [347.302]   91-33886

British Library Cataloguing in Publication Data is available.

Copyright © 1992 by Barbara M. Yarnold

Library of Congress Catalog Card Number: 91-33886
ISBN: 0-275-94166-3

First published in 1992

Praeger Publishers, One Madison Avenue, New York, NY 10010
An imprint of Greenwood Publishing Group, Inc.

Printed in the United States of America

⬯

The paper used in this book complies with the
Permanent Paper Standard issued by the National
Information Standards Organization (Z39.48-1984).

10 9 8 7 6 5 4 3 2 1

To the poor and noble,
including many members
of the Suszko and Yarnold families.

Contents

Tables   ix

Preface   xi

Introduction   xiii

Part I
Political versus Contextual Variables: Do Law and Facts Count?

1   Why Judges Are Not Constrained by Law and Facts   3

2   When Do Political Factors Affect Judicial Decision Making?   7

3   Contextual Variables: Region   53

Part II
Judicial versus Administrative Decision Making

4   Comparing Judicial and Administrative Decision Making   71

5   A Synthesis and a General Model   103

Part III

New Approaches: Combining Public Law with Pluralism and Theories about Social Movements

6   Social Movements and Public Interest
    Litigation Groups   109

Bibliography   129

Index   141

Tables

2.1   Probit Estimates for Federal District Court and
       Court of Appeals Determinations in Asylum-Related
       Appeals, 1980–87   21

2.2   Regression Estimates for State Court Sentencing
       Decisions in Rape Cases, 1987–89   31

2.3   Regression Estimates for State Court Sentencing
       Decisions in Rape Cases, 1987–89   32

2.4   Probit Estimates for Federal District Court
       Determinations in Extradition Cases, 1932–90   40

2.5   Probit Estimates for Federal District Court
       Determinations in Extradition Cases, 1932–90   41

3.1   Probit Estimates for District Court Abortion
       Cases, 1973–90   61

4.1   Probit Estimates for BIA Determinations in
       Asylum-Related Appeals, 1980–87   82

4.2   Probit Estimates for Federal District and Court
       of Appeals Determinations in Asylum-Related
       Appeals, 1980–87   83

Preface

I would like to sincerely thank those who made this work possible. In graduate school, I was fortunate to work with two inspiring political scientists, Andrew McFarland and Lettie Wenner. I received a doctoral degree in public policy analysis/political science in 1988 from the University of Illinois at Chicago.

I drafted most of this book in my first year as an assistant professor of public administration at Florida International University, in North Miami, Florida. The reduced teaching load (two courses per semester) assisted me enormously in this endeavor, as did other material resources and the positive reinforcement of Dr. Allan Rosenbaum, dean of the School of Public Affairs; Dr. Harvey Averch, chairman of the department of public administration; the support staff at the university; and my friends and colleagues. Pauline M. Broderick also tirelessly and enthusiastically prepared an excellent index for this text.

Of course, I would not have embarked on this work had I not been motivated by love for humanity. To a great extent, I owe this to my family: Helen Marie Yarnold, my mother; Irena Maria Suszko, my aunt; Susan Maria Yarnold, my sister; and my brothers, Paul Richard Yarnold, Ph.D., Charles Nicholas Yarnold, James Alexander Yarnold, and Jack Christopher Yarnold.

Also, I dedicate this to the memory of my deceased father, James Knapps Yarnold, Ph.D., a dedicated father and scholar; and to my deceased grandparents, especially Stanislawa and Micolaj Suszko, who labored intensely so that their grandchildren might have a glimpse of hope.

Introduction

IN SEARCH OF A THEORY OF PUBLIC LAW

As a graduate student in public policy analysis/political science under the precise direction of Lettie M. Wenner, a prominent public law researcher, I recall being somewhat bewildered by the numerous conflicting results of public law analyses, which seemed to lack cohesion. Research efforts to that point were quite impressive in terms of their contribution to understanding decision making by the courts. As an attorney who had practiced law and served as a law clerk to a state court judge (civil division), many of the attacks of public law analysts on the presumed objectivity and impartiality of the courts seemed justified to me.

Any law student who has suffered through three years of examinations that require erudite comprehension of the law, and who has spent countless hours reading through cases in search of the law, has some intuitive sense that the great cases that are important precedents (primarily U.S. Supreme Court cases) lack internal consistency and meaning, and are perhaps molded not so much by enlightened constitutional analysis as by the political and cultural environment of presiding judges and their personal preferences.

My subsequent practice as an attorney tended to confirm these early suspicions, as I observed that the best attorneys are those who are able to win the "unwinnable" cases, in which both the facts and the law appear to offer little support to their clients. Further, the most successful attorneys seem to spend more time on their yachts, playing golf, and driving European cars than their less successful counterparts, who are often found madly searching for the law in law libraries. In short, some of the best attorneys seemed to prosper not so much due to their intellectual powers as due to their awareness of court politics. These are the lawyers who know where to file a particular case and which judge might be most inclined to rule in their favor. They invest time and energy in maintaining personal and professional ties to the judiciary and other elite members of the legal community.

Hence, the open challenge made by public law researchers to the "law school model" of judicial decision making, which suggests courts objectively apply the knowable law to the clear facts of a case in order to reach an objective decision, had obvious appeal. Nevertheless, research in the public law area was itself somewhat bewildering. Research efforts approached their analysis of court decision making through the use of a multitude of different data, research methods, and statistical analyses. Some researchers confined themselves to explaining court outcomes in terms of judicial values and role orientations, while others examined various elements of the "judicial environment." Some researchers (without express acknowledgment) went far outside the domain of political science in order to explain court outcomes. For example, such research on court decision making has utilized variables drawn from psychology, economics, criminal justice, and sociology.

The underlying uniformity in the public law area, nevertheless, seems to be an acknowledgment that judicial decision making is not always objective, that courts are not unduly constrained by the law and the facts of a case, and that courts are policy makers, influenced by extraneous factors that may have little to do with the legal and factual elements of a case.

CHAPTER OUTLINE

In an attempt to instill some intellectual order in my own house, my public law research, although involving different substantive areas, has been somewhat preoccupied with the underlying question posed in Part I: When are political and environmental variables related to judicial decision making? Or do the law and facts of a case count?

Chapter 1 suggests, first, that judges are relatively unconstrained by the law and facts of cases and that the excess discretion that results is often used for judicial policy making. Chapter 2 focuses on the issue of political factors that are related to court outcomes. It includes three case studies. Case Study 1 (asylum-related appeals to the federal courts) and Case Study 3 (federal district court international extradition cases) find that political factors are related to outcome. Case Study 2, in contrast, finds that political factors were not related to outcome in state court rape-sentencing cases.

Chapter 3 is entitled "Contextual Factors: Region." Included in this chapter is Case Study 4, a public law analysis of judicial decision making in federal district court abortion cases that finds that regional variables are significantly related to outcome.

Part II, "Judicial Versus Administrative Decision Making," continues the inquiry into the influence of political factors on judicial decision making. It does this by comparing decisions in asylum-related appeals by two different types of decision makers: an administrative appeals board and the federal courts (Chapter 4, Case Study 5). It finds that political factors influenced both types of decision makers, but that the political factors related to outcome differed. While the federal courts responded to the involvement of interest groups in litigation, this variable was not significant in the administrative context. Instead, decisions by the administrative tribunal in question were related to the biases of the immigration bureaucracy and the foreign policy directives of the U.S. State Department. This suggests that although outcomes in both contexts are politicized, agency and judicial decision makers respond to the beat of different political drummers.

Chapter 5 reviews the preceding analyses and devises a general model of public law that suggests, in summary form, when political and regional factors are likely to be related to judicial decision making.

Part III, "New Approaches: Combining Public Law with Pluralism and Theories about Social Movements," represents an explicit recognition of the multidisciplinary nature of public law research and suggests one of a multitude of these approaches. Chapter 6 (Case Study 6), "Social Movements and Public Interest Litigation Groups," examines these trends in the context of the U.S. sanctuary movement.

I

Political versus Contextual Variables: Do Law and Facts Count?

1

Why Judges Are Not Constrained by Law and Facts

The "law school model" of judicial decision making, still an implicit core of legal education in the United States, was developed in an attempt to instill the scientific process into the legal discipline. According to this model, judges objectively apply the law to the facts of a case in order to reach a decision that is impartial and apolitical. Judges are socialized into this model of decision making and apply it rigorously after they ascend the bench, with the result that uniform fact patterns yield uniform judicial decisions (Glick, 1983). At the core of this model is the concept that judges do not actively make public policy.

As is often the case, it is quite difficult to have much success when scientific models are applied to human activity. This is particularly true when one deals with the legal system, which is designed to both constrain human activity and protect fundamental individual rights. The legal system is designed to encourage appropriate human activity within certain amorphous confines and is administered by humans: Judges, lawyers, and court personnel all interact to affect judicial decisions. The main philosophical underpinnings of the legal system have been derived from the dictates of a dominant Judeo-Christian culture and secular philosophers generally associated with Western civilization. Hence, the concept of a legal system is at odds with a scientific model that attempts to base all activity on positive rational models.

For example, the decision to maintain a society with rules and courts in which disputes are resolved through the legal system instead of through the use of force is itself a subjective decision about the desirability of maintaining such a system. Certainly some groups, including primitive civilizations and anarchists, do not agree that such an ordered way of resolving disputes is either necessary or desirable. Further, the reliance on humans as litigants, lawyers, and judges is essentially a decision that human concerns are important to a political system and that they are best resolved by humans with similar backgrounds, cultural values, and expectations.

Nevertheless, it is necessary, particularly when one is confronted by a branch of government that is deprived of enforcement machinery and relies a great deal for compliance on voluntary activity of corporations, individuals, and public officials, that the courts somehow maintain a high degree of legitimacy. One way to accomplish this is to adopt symbols for the judiciary. The essential ones are the objectivity and impartiality of judges, their independence from political encroachments, and their non-involvement in policy making (other, more superficial symbols include, for example, the long robes worn by judges, the austere formality of courtrooms, and the reference to judges as "your honor").

Nevertheless, the research of public law analysts has repeatedly challenged the underlying concept of judicial objectivity. In contrast to traditional models of judges as passive interpreters of the law, numerous analysts have discovered that judges are relatively unconstrained in their decision making by the law and the facts of a case due to the underlying vagueness of the law and uncertainty in terms of objective, knowable laws.

Frank (1978), for example, asserts that the law school model of judicial decision making is flawed since the "facts" on which judges rely are actually guesses arrived at through an adversarial process in which opposing sides are motivated to present only arguments favorable to one side. Courts do not engage in independent investigations to discover the facts of a case but rely on evidence provided by litigants. Facts may be forgotten or omitted, and parties may misrepresent the facts. In cases that require factual determinations based on scientific or technological expertise, the situation is even worse as judges lose their ability to make a "reasonable man" determination as to the facts of a case. In these cases, courts tend to be entirely dependent on expert testimony, provided by self-serving litigants (Blank 1984).

The law school model of judicial decision making also incorrectly assumes that judges are restrained in their decision making by objective, clear laws. This model incorrectly assumes that the law (including statutes, judicial precedents, constitutional provisions, and regulations) that is applied by judges is uniform in cases that have similar facts. Glick (1983) and others assert that judges are not at all certain about which law applies in a given case. Attorneys involved in litigation attempt to convince judges that the laws that apply are those that favor their clients. In fact, if they fail to vigorously make such an argument, they may be subject to malpractice suits.

If there were agreement on which law applies in a given case, there would be no need for a whole tier of appeals courts, which exists for the main purpose of correcting the errors of lower court judges in their application and interpretation of the law. If the law that applied in a given case were always certain and knowable, lower court judges would not be reversed on appeal on the basis that they either misapplied or misconstrued applicable laws (Yarnold 1990b). Instead, in a world of legal uncertainty, their decisions are routinely reversed for precisely this reason.

In my own public law research, some of which is set forth in the following chapters, I repeatedly observed that courts were relatively unconstrained in their decision making by the law because the standards they were called on to interpret were vague. In Chapter 2, Case Study 1 (on federal court outcomes in asylum-related appeals), judges were called on to determine whether political refugees had met the "well-founded fear of persecution" test for political asylum and the "clear probability of persecution" test for withholding of deportation, a task made particularly difficult since there is no commonly accepted definition of "persecution," the core requirement for both claims.

Vague legal standards also appear in the other analyses. In Chapter 2, Case Study 2, district court judges in Montana were given virtually no statutory direction in their sentencing of convicted rapists, in terms of the length of the sentences and in their decisions to suspend or defer sentences. In international extradition cases (Chapter 2, Case Study 3), legal standards are nonexistent or vague; those that exist are often derived from antiquated U.S. Supreme Court decisions. Adding to the complexity in international extradition proceedings is that the law that applies is set forth in over 100 bilateral extradition treaties that the United States has entered into with other countries (Hall 1987; Kester 1988). Similarly, district court judges that dealt with the issue of abortion (Chapter 3, Case Study 4) in the aftermath of the Supreme Court's decision in *Roe v. Wade* (1973) were faced with applying quite vague legal standards, based on disputed biological fact, the interpretation of which is still a subject of lively debate.

IMPLICATIONS: COURTS AS POLICY MAKERS

Since judges are often unconstrained by the law and facts of a case, they wield considerable discretion and are properly viewed as policy makers. Hence, judicial decisions may be related to extraneous variables.

Public law researchers have been quite creative in their search for variables that affect judicial decision making. Some variables that surface in public law analyses include the geographic region of judges (Wenner 1982; Wenner and Dutter 1988); the political culture of a judge's geographical area (Levin 1978); a judge's background (Goldman 1975); judicial attitudes and values (Spaeth 1981; Pritchett 1978; Danelski 1981); judicial role perceptions (Beiser 1978; Howard 1978); small group interaction (Danelski 1978; Murphy 1981; Ulmer 1981); and the personal qualifications of attorneys involved in litigation (Jacob 1981; Casper 1981).

My research tends to focus on political factors, including the partisanship of judges or their appointing presidents, the involvement of interest groups in litigation, and the preferences of judicial constituencies, defined as those individuals in a judge's geographical area who are most likely to be directly affected by the decision in question.

Perhaps the best illustration of the policy-making roles of courts is the fact that the Supreme Court has varied in terms of its treatment of individual rights and that the variation in its decision making is based on changes in presiding justices, political and environmental conditions, and public opinion. Baum (1989), for example, suggests that the Supreme Court was an advocate of business interests during the period of 1865 to 1937, when it typically held that government regulation of business violated the "contracts" clause or the "due process" clause of the U.S. Constitution.

The Supreme Court's position changed fundamentally after it closed ranks with Congress and President Franklin Roosevelt over the president's New Deal program, which was designed to lift the nation out of the Great Depression. In 1935 and 1936, the Supreme Court handed down decisions that nearly dealt a death blow to early New Deal legislation.

These decisions led to intense criticism of the Court and gave birth to a plan to increase the Court's size to fifteen members, which would permit Roosevelt to pack the Court with friendly justices. Although the plan ultimately failed to pass Congress, in a series of decisions entered in 1937, the Supreme Court gave its support to New Deal laws. One justice retired shortly thereafter and others left the court within a short time, allowing Roosevelt to fill the vacant positions with supporters of his programs. Since 1937, the Supreme Court has been noted for its support of civil liberties (Baum 1989).

Although much attention in public law research is focused on the Supreme Court, lower federal courts operate under similar conditions, relatively unconstrained by the law and the facts of individual cases. They wield enormous discretion in their decision making and often actively embrace their policy-making function. The following chapters examine judicial policy making in asylum-related appeals (Chapter 2, Case Study 1), rape sentencing decisions (Chapter 2, Case Study 2), international extradition proceedings (Chapter 2, Case Study 3), and abortion cases (Chapter 3, Case Study 4).

2

When Do Political Factors Affect Judicial Decision Making?

In the attempt to set forth a general theory of public law, one of the first questions that must be addressed is: Under what conditions is it most probable that a particular variable will be significantly related to judicial outcomes? My observations of public law research led me to believe that, in spite of the apparent contradictions that exist in the analyses, there might still be an underlying thread that links cases into broad categories. Chapter 1 set forth the essential premise that judges are most often unconstrained by the law and facts of a case since laws are vague and facts are uncertain. Under these circumstances, courts wield great discretion and may be influenced by extraneous variables. This chapter begins the quest for a general theory of public law with the question of when political factors affect judicial decision making.

IDENTIFYING RELEVANT POLITICAL FACTORS

Before addressing the broader question of when political factors affect judicial decision making, it is necessary to identify relevant political factors. Directly opposing the traditional view of the federal judiciary as apolitical, which arises from the fact that these judges are appointed rather than elected, previous public law research has repeatedly shown that judges are influenced in their decision making by political variables (Cook 1981; Wenner 1982; Wenner and Dutter 1988; Baum 1989; Yarnold 1990a, 1990b, 1991). Although many political variables have been raised in public law analyses, I intend to focus on the following:

Political Party

One of the most conspicuous and important features of U.S. politics is the fact that it is dominated by a two-party system, with political "spoils" and power divided between the Democratic and Republican parties. These parties represent broad segments of the U.S. public; the Democratic party has traditionally been allied with organized labor, middle- and lower-income wage earners, and immigrants. More recently, it has also taken on the representation of women, blacks, and other minorities. In contrast, the Republican party has been the voice of business interests and upper-class wage earners (Cummings and Wise 1985; Schattshneider 1960).

If judges are influenced by their political environment, perhaps they are influenced in their decision making in individual cases by their own political party affiliations or by the partisan affiliations of the president who appointed them (Baum 1989; Goldman 1975; Nagel 1961; Vines 1963; Yarnold 1990a, 1990b, 1991; Carp and Rowland 1983).

Judicial Constituencies and Public Opinion

Another political variable that may affect judicial decision making is public opinion (Cook 1981; Baum 1989) or the preferences of what I have referred to as judicial constituencies (Yarnold 1990a, 1990b, 1991). Judicial constituents are those individuals or groups within judges' areas (whether these are districts, circuits, counties, or states) that are most likely to be directly affected by the judicial decision in question. Hence, for example, in asylum-related appeals (Case Study 1, Chapter 2), the judicial constituency of judges is identified as the immigrant population within judges' areas, since immigrants are most likely to be directly affected by the decisions in cases involving political refugees and asylees.

The judicial constituency of judges is likely to change as courts shift their attention from one litigation issue to another. Hence, in rape sentencing cases (Case Study 2, Chapter 2), immigrants are not likely to be directly affected by these decisions. The judicial constituency identified in rape cases is politically powerful women within county government. It is predicted that judges respond in individual cases to the preferences of their judicial constituents.

Interest Group Litigation

Although interest groups are unable to engage in certain lobbying activities when it comes to the courts (for example, giving campaign contributions and meeting with judges when cases are pending before them), they are able to lobby the courts through interest group litigation. Another political variable that many suggest influences judicial decision making is interest group litigation or the involvement of organized interests in litigation, whether they appear as representatives of individuals or as *amicus curiae* (Galanter 1974, 1978; Dolbeare

1978; Epstein 1985; Wenner 1982; Wenner and Dutter 1988; Yarnold 1990a, 1990b, 1991). The prediction is that litigants who are either represented by an interest group or have interest groups bolstering their arguments through *amicus curiae* appearances will tend to be more successful than litigants without the benefit of interest group litigation.

WHY SHOULD JUDGES RESPOND TO POLITICS?

It was earlier argued that "the link to the political environment is even greater for federal court judges than for most citizens" (Yarnold 1990a). One reason for this statement is that federal court judges tend to be political activists in U.S. politics. Lawrence Baum (1989) points out that federal court judges have often, prior to their appointment to the federal bench, held positions as state court judges or administrators. Many have also held elective political office. They have been conditioned, even after their appointment to the federal courts, to serve as political actors, that is, to be responsive to the subtle pressures from their political environment.

Another factor that links federal court judges to their political context is that they have often been involved in partisan politics prior to their appointment, and the partisan affiliations of judges is an important criterion in the selection process (Goldman 1975; Nagel 1961; Vines 1963; Carp and Rowland 1983).

My addition to the discussion is that federal court judges may be responsive to political factors in their decision making in individual cases "due to the prospect of future promotion within the ranks of the judiciary or appointment to administrative positions" (Yarnold 1990a). One assessment of federal court judges, based on their careers prior to their appointment to the federal bench, is that they appear to have high levels of both ambition and energy. Given this, it is unreasonable to assume that once they reach federal judicial office below the level of the U.S. Supreme Court, their ambition will suddenly subside.

Instead, it is argued that federal court judges decide cases with a view to future advancement within the judiciary or appointment to desirable positions outside of the judiciary. Hence, cases that come before judges are evaluated in terms of their political effects; for example, whether it is possible that a decision in a particular case will alienate a significant judicial constituency.

For example, in asylum-related appeals to the federal courts (Case Study 1, Chapter 2), federal court judges in areas that had a high percentage of immigrants (or high immigrant flow) were more inclined to rule in favor of litigants who claimed they were refugees than judges in areas with low immigrant flows. Along similar lines, Baum (1989) suggests that courts are unlikely to adopt policies that fail to maintain minimum levels of social support. Cook (1981) found that sentencing decisions of federal court judges in draft cases were related to public opinion.

Of course, this is not to intended to paint a picture of a sinister, scheming, federal judiciary. Some judges are more prone to political influences than others. Caldeira (1981), for example, suggests that judges respond to different incentives. Political calculations by federal court judges may go on without the express knowledge of the judges involved in litigation. Rather, the political calculations of federal court judges may be the product of subtle unconscious assessments of the demands of their political environment—an environment they have become quite sensitive to as a result of their political pasts.

Another reason that federal court judges respond to political stimuli is that political actors become involved in federal court litigation. For example, many analysts have documented the involvement of interest groups in litigation and the fact that interest groups generally tend to have higher levels of success in litigation than nonorganizational litigants (Galanter 1974, 1978; Dolbeare 1978; Epstein 1985; Wenner 1982; Wenner and Dutter 1988; Yarnold 1990a, 1990b, 1991). Although somewhat circumscribed in their lobbying activities (they cannot, for example, give financial contributions to federal court judges or have *ex parte* communications with them), interest groups lobby the federal judiciary by becoming involved in cases presided over by federal court judges (Baum 1989).

In the analysis of federal court outcomes in asylum-related appeals (Case Study 1, Chapter 2), it is posited that the involvement of interest groups might lead to high levels of litigation success for two reasons: (1) because organizations have superior litigation resources with which to argue the merits of a case (Galanter, 1974, 1978); and (2) because federal court judges respond to the political clout of these organizations.

In Case Study 3, Chapter 2, in which federal court judges made decisions in cases involving international extradition, no organizations appeared on the behalf of litigants subject to international extradition proceedings (referred to as "relators"). Since the litigation resources of interest groups are not relevant, this case study presents an excellent test of the extent to which federal court judges respond to the political clout of organizations linked to litigation.

The analysis confirms that federal court judges tended to respond to the political clout of important groups and ethnic lobbies in these cases, as relators linked to the strong Irish lobby in the United States tended to win in these cases at a much higher rate than did relators linked to no organization or a weak organization, such as their Palestine Liberation Organization, which lacks the support of a strong ethnic lobby in the United States.

Other political actors that often become involved in federal court cases are agents of executive and legislative branches of government, such as the Immigration and Naturalization Service and the Internal Revenue Service. Officials of federal, state, and local government may become involved as plaintiffs or defendants in federal court cases (Baum 1989).

Having thus identified political factors that may affect judicial decision making and some of the motives for politicized judicial decision making, we may now proceed to examine individual case studies.

CASE STUDY 1: WHEN JUDGES BEND TO
POLITICAL PRESSURE

Federal Court Outcomes in Asylum-Related Appeals
1980–87: A Highly "Politicized" Process

In spite of attempts to shield the federal judiciary from political influences, federal judges still play a significant role in asylum-related appeals. This has the unfortunate effect that congressional policy goals in the asylum policy area are subordinated to political considerations. This analysis finds that applicants for asylum and/or withholding are more likely to prevail in their appeals to the federal courts if they are represented by an organization or have an organization arguing on their behalf as *amicus curiae*. They are also more likely to prevail in their appeals if the judges involved in the case were appointed by a Democratic president and if there is a high immigrant flow into their areas. Thus, as federal court judges respond to their constituencies, the partisanship of their appointing presidents, and organizational involvement in the appeals, an ostensibly humanitarian asylum policy is distorted as the merits of individual claims for asylum and withholding become less important than the political variables involved in a particular case.

Many other analysts have also found that judicial decision making, both at the state and federal levels, is influenced by political variables (Baum 1989; Wenner 1982; Levin 1978; Cook 1981). Hence, the concept of the judiciary as an apolitical branch of government has been, for the most part, discarded. However, much of the research on the judiciary has been characterized by some of the following types of problems: (1) the analysis is qualitative in nature; (2) the analysis fails to explain sufficiently why judicial decision making is politicized; (3) the analysis fails to take into account more than one political variable that may have influenced judicial decision making; and (4) the analysis fails to consider (and to control for) the effects of other, non-political variables that have been shown to have an important impact on policy making by the judiciary and by decision makers within the overtly political branches (executive and legislative). Such variables include, for example, the region of the country of the decision maker (Wenner 1982; Wenner and Dutter 1988; Carp and Rowland 1983; Richardson and Vines 1978) and economic conditions at the time of (or shortly prior to) decision making. Fifth, the analysis fails to consider that certain political and/or contextual variables may be significant only in certain limited policy areas and not in others. For example, region as a variable may be significantly related to judicial decision making in a highly ideological case, such as one involving race relations. However, region may not be significantly related to outcome when the case is more ideologically neutral, such as a mortgage foreclosure action, in which other variables, such as the state of the economy and interest group litigation, may be more significantly related to judicial decision making.

This research attempts to address some of these earlier difficulties through multivariate analysis of decision making by the federal courts in appeals from adverse administrative decisions on claims for asylum and withholding of deportation (two remedies in U.S. immigration laws that allow aliens to remain in the United States because they fear persecution in their countries of origin).

Traditionalists suggest that the judicial branch of the federal government is not influenced by political factors since federal court judges are appointed and not elected. This creates the expectation that the federal judiciary consists of independent, objective decision makers (Glick 1983). The law school model of decision making posits that judges reach decisions in a mechanistic manner, applying the law to the facts of a case in order to reach a decision. Judges serve merely to apply the objective, knowable law to actual disputes.

Simon (1957; Simon, Smithburg, and Thompson 1962) and others discredited such rigid decision-making models for administrative agencies, finding that decision rules given to agencies by, for example, enabling statutes, are often unclear and conflicting. When administrators attempt to simply implement policy goals, they are often unable to decipher the meaning of those policy goals. Given this ambiguity, administrators have a great deal of discretion in their implementation of policy programs and usually develop their own decision rules, which may not coincide with, for example, congressional policy goals. Administrative decision makers thus engage in the formation and not just the implementation of policy.

Similarly, the law school model of judicial decision making has fallen into disfavor, largely due to the realization that neither the law nor the facts that judges rely on are objective or knowable. Frank (1978) suggests that the facts on which judges rely are more like guesses, arrived at through an adversarial process in which litigants have great incentive to mold the facts to their advantage. Facts are forgotten or omitted, and litigants may misrepresent the facts. Similarly, the law that judges are to apply is not objective. Statutes that must be construed by judges are (as in the administrative context) vague and contain conflicting policy goals. Previous cases (or precedent) relied on by judges may also be an unreliable guide to the law. It may not be clear whether a previous case is applicable (it may be, for example, distinguishable on the facts), and it may be difficult to identify the holding of a case. Due to the fact that both the law and the facts that apply in a given case are not clear, judges are often left without definite decision rules and must develop their own. Hence, judges do more than simply interpret the law in specific factual disputes. Like administrative decision makers, judges wield a great deal of discretion in their decision making and are properly viewed as policy makers.

Given that judges are policy makers, the question then becomes: Which variables influence federal court decision making? Recalling from the previous discussion that the answer to this question may depend on the type of case being examined (for example, civil rights or environmental), it is necessary to introduce the substantive policy area with which judges are concerned in this analysis.

Asylum-Related Appeals to the Federal Courts

Most immigrants to the United States come for the purpose of employment or family reunification. However, a subgroup of immigrants, referred to as refugees, seek to reside in the United States because they fear persecution in their countries of origin. There are two categories of refugees: those who file their applications when they are outside of the United States (referred to as "refugees") and those who seek to gain refugee status after they have arrived in the United States (referred to as "asylees"). Asylees file their applications in the United States.

The focus in this analysis of federal court decision making is on asylum policy, which includes decisions relating to both political asylum and withholding of deportation. These two mechanisms allow refugees who are in the United States or are at a port of entry to remain in the United States if they have a well-founded fear of persecution (asylum), or if there exists a clear probability of persecution if they are deported (withholding of deportation). It is the responsibility of federal court judges to determine whether administrative officials properly applied these vague standards in individual cases before them. For the purpose of this analysis, "asylum-related cases and appeals" include cases and appeals that involve claims (by an alien) for either asylum or withholding.

Although refugees (outside of the United States) have been admitted for some time, 1980 was the first year in which the United States allowed aliens already in the country to apply for political asylum. This was accomplished with passage of the Refugee Act of 1980. In addition to providing for asylum, the act also sought to rid refugee and asylum policy of a long-term bias in favor of aliens from so-called hostile countries, or countries with communist, socialist, or leftist forms of government. The act ostensibly accomplished this through redefining the term "refugee," previously defined as a person from a communist country or the Middle East, to mean

> any person who is outside any country of such person's nationality, or in
> the case of a person having no nationality, is outside any country in which
> such person last habitually resided, and who is unable to avail himself
> or herself of the protection of that country because of persecution or a
> well-founded fear of persecution on account of race, religion, nationality,
> membership in a particular social group, or political opinion. (Refugee Act
> of 1980, Section 208(a))

Regulations provide three routes through which an alien may obtain political asylum. First, an alien may file an application for asylum with a district office of the Immigration and Naturalization Service (INS) if the alien is in the United States and neither exclusion nor deportation proceedings have been initiated.

Second, in the event that this application for asylum is unsuccessful, the alien may, in a subsequent exclusion or deportation hearing, resubmit the request for asylum to an immigration judge. Third, the alien may request asylum for the first time during the course of an exclusion or deportation proceeding.

Aliens may appeal adverse determinations of immigration judges on their claims for asylum and withholding. If an asylum claim is raised during the course of a deportation proceeding and is denied, administrative review is to the Board of Immigration Appeals (BIA), and subsequent judicial review is to the federal courts of appeal. If an asylum claim is raised during the course of an exclusion proceeding and is denied, administrative review is again to the BIA; however, subsequent judicial review is to the federal district courts, through a *habeas corpus* petition. The ruling of a district court on a *habeas corpus* petition may thereafter be appealed to the federal courts of appeal.

A limited form of asylum has existed in U.S. law since passage of the Immigration and Nationality Act of 1952; this is referred to as "withholding of deportation." Initially, severe restrictions were placed on eligibility for withholding. Subsequent amendments to the act substantially broadened this provision, and current legislation prevents the attorney general from deporting an alien who faces a "clear possibility" of persecution on account of race, religion, nationality, membership in a particular social group, or political opinion (Section 243(h) of the 1952 Immigration and Nationality Act). An application for withholding of deportation may be raised in the course of both exclusion and deportation hearings. Appeals from adverse orders of immigration judges on requests for withholding follow the same route as appeals in asylum cases.

Hypotheses

In contrast to the traditional model of the judiciary as a passive interpreter of the law, judges examined in this analysis were relatively unconstrained by the law in their decision making, because the standards they were called on to interpret were vague. In cases involving withholding of deportation, the courts were concerned with whether the BIA and immigration judges properly found that an alien did or did not face a "clear probability" of persecution. Similarly, in appeals involving claims for asylum, the applicable standard was a "well-founded fear" of persecution. Many immigration experts have commented on the ambiguity of these terms and the apparent arbitrariness of decisions made by both administrative and judicial decision makers when called on to apply these standards. Blum (1986) suggests, for example, that the standards do not indicate to an alien how much and what kind of evidence he or she is required to provide, and what criteria the trier of fact and the reviewing court should use in analyzing the evidence. Edwards (1983) concludes that the standards contain both objective and subjective elements and that it is difficult to determine the meaning of either standard. Hyndman (1986) adds that ambiguity is added to the analysis since there is no commonly accepted definition of persecution, the core requirement for both asylum and withholding claims.

It should come as no surprise, given the vagueness of the underlying standards for asylum and withholding, that administrative and judicial decisions on both types of claims have been attacked as arbitrary and, in some cases, even biased in favor of certain groups. Particularly with respect to administrative decision making on asylum-related claims, numerous critics have attacked the agencies involved (including the INS, immigration judges, the BIA, and the State Department, through its issuance of advisory opinions in these cases) for employing inappropriate criteria in their asylum-related determinations. Specifically, critics charge that administrative agencies have, since World War II, consistently favored in refugee and asylum decisions aliens from countries with communist, socialist, and leftist forms of government (referred to as "hostile" countries). They suggest that this bias has been perpetuated by the administrative agencies in spite of the Refugee Act of 1980, which was intended to eliminate this bias through its expanded definition of "refugee" (Loescher and Scanlan 1986; Helton 1984; Parker 1985; Van Der Hout 1985; Preston 1986). Hence, following legislation that presumably eliminated the hostile country bias, aliens fleeing from, for example, the Eastern bloc countries of Poland and Russia are more likely to have their claims for asylum and withholding of deportation approved by agencies within the immigration bureaucracy than are aliens from non-hostile countries such as El Salvador and Haiti.

Just as administrative agencies are able to exercise great discretion in their decision making on asylum-related claims, one expects that the federal courts may be similarly unconstrained in their decision making. As a result of increased discretion, agencies are able to substitute their own goals for statutory goals; while the Refugee Act of 1980 called for a depoliticization of asylum-related determinations, administrative agencies continue to promote a foreign policy goal of favoring hostile-country aliens over aliens from non-hostile countries. It is not expected that the federal courts, like administrative decision makers below, will favor in asylum-related appeal aliens from hostile countries. The federal courts are, after all, independent of the immigration bureaucracy and are expected to correct agency abuses. However, to the extent that administrative agencies are able to substitute their own goals for vague policy goals set forth in standards for asylum and withholding, one anticipates that federal court outcomes may also have been related to extraneous (or non-legal) variables. The following discussion reviews the extraneous independent variables that are examined in this analysis.

Political Variables

A category of extraneous variables that may be significantly related to federal court decision making in asylum-related appeals includes political variables. A newcomer to this area might find this suggestion somewhat anomalous, given that the federal courts are generally viewed as independent of political influences because their members are appointed, not elected. However, in the same way that courts have been "unclothed" with respect to their policy making role, many analysts concede that judicial decision making is often related to political factors. This is not a complete surprise: Judges do not operate in a vacuum and may be influenced by their environment, including their political environment.

Political Party. If judges are influenced by political variables, one of the most prominent features of the U.S. political system is the presence of two major political parties: Democratic and Republican. Perhaps federal court judges are influenced in their decision making by the political party affiliation of the president who appointed them. It is predicted that aliens will more likely prevail in their asylum-related appeals to the federal courts when the judge or judges involved in a case were appointed by a Democratic president.

Public Opinion. Another political variable that may affect federal court judges is public opinion or the preferences of their constituents.

In evaluating the link between policy making and constituency preferences, one must address the question of which constituency of the decision maker might be most directly influenced by the decision in question. In the asylum policy area, the constituency most likely to be affected include those who seek to gain political asylum, and, more generally, immigrants. Immigrants may be a significant judicial constituency in the asylum policy area; the presence of a sizable immigrant population in a judge's circuit may affect a judge's decision in an asylum-related appeal. One way to assess the size of the immigrant population in judicial circuits is to measure the annual immigrant flow into the circuit of each judge relative to the circuit's total population. A specific hypothesis is that federal court judges from high immigrant flow circuits will more likely decide in favor of aliens in asylum-related appeals than will judges in low immigrant flow circuits.

Interest Group Litigation. Although interest groups are constrained from most lobbying activities when it comes to the courts (for example, giving campaign contributions and meeting with judges), they are able to lobby the courts through interest group litigation. Thus, another political variable that many suggest influences judicial decision making is interest group litigation, or the involvement of organized interests in litigation. A third hypothesis is that interest group involvement in asylum-related appeals is significantly related to outcome in these cases. Specifically, aliens who are either represented by organizations in these appeals or have organizations arguing on their behalf as *amicus curiae* will more often prevail in these appeals than will aliens who either appear *pro se* or are represented by a private attorney.

Competing Hypotheses

Other analysts agree that the federal courts are policy makers but do not believe that political factors alone are sufficient to explain court outcomes. Instead, they often point to contextual or environmental variables as significantly related to judicial decision making.

Region. One contextual variable thought to affect court decision making is the region in which a decision maker is located (Carp and Rowland 1983; Wenner

1982; Wenner and Dutter 1988). Carp and Rowland (1983) showed that federal district court judges in the South and West were more conservative in their decision making than judges in the North and Midwest. Richardson and Vines (1978) found that both the U.S. Department of Justice and civil rights litigants encountered, in their civil rights litigation, the greatest resistance from district courts in the deep South. Similarly, in her analysis of the sentencing behavior of federal district court judges, Cook (1977) claims that "severe judges" tend to sit in districts in the South. Wenner (1982) found that geographic location influenced both congressmen and federal court judges in their consideration of environmental issues. In their subsequent analysis, Wenner and Dutter (1988) supported the earlier observation with a finding that federal court judges in Southern circuits, during the period 1970–85, tended to decide environmental cases in favor of industry and against environmental groups; so also did judges from the 10th circuit, located in the West. In district court cases, judges in Northeastern circuits (circuits 1, 2, and 3) had the highest level of support for environmental groups, followed, in descending order, by judges in the Midwest (circuits 6, 7, and 8) and in the South (circuits 4, 5, and 11). Judges in circuits in the West (circuits 9 and 10) were divided.

Hence, a competing hypothesis is that the decisions of the federal courts in asylum-related appeals are significantly related to region. Since this factor has so often been cited in explaining court outcomes, it should properly be included as a control variable.

Unemployment Rate. Other contextualist political scientists, including Dye (1966) and perhaps Hofferbert (1974), might agree with the suggestion of numerous economists that U.S. refugee policy, as a subgroup of general U.S. immigration policy, is influenced by economic conditions in the United States, particularly by the unemployment rate (Briggs 1984; Loescher and Scanlan 1986; Chiswick 1981, 1986). A second competing hypothesis is that federal court outcomes in asylum-related appeals are significantly related to the unemployment rate in the United States shortly prior to the time that the appeals were decided.

European and Hostile Country Bias. Critics of U.S. refugee and asylum policy contend that it contains two biases: (1) a bias in favor of aliens from hostile countries; and (2) a bias in favor of aliens from European countries (Loescher and Scanlan 1986; Preston 1986). With regard to the first bias, in favor of hostile-country aliens, inclusion of this variable will allow us to ascertain whether the federal courts, in deciding asylum-related appeals, serve to perpetuate administrative practices or are perhaps influenced by other variables.

Data and Methods

Data for this analysis consist of all published decisions in asylum-related appeals appearing in reporters for both federal district court decisions (*Federal Supplement*) and federal courts of appeal (*Federal Reporter*) for the period of January 1, 1980, to September 1, 1987. There are 146 asylum-related appeals.

Certain methodological problems arise with regard to the data. First, the court decisions published in the official reporters represent a small portion of actual decisions by the federal courts in asylum-related appeals. Further, the decisions that are published are not always selected for their importance in setting legal precedents but are published simply because the judge or judges involved in the case had the initiative to submit them for publication. The decisions published may therefore not be a fair representation of the population of all such decisions. Nevertheless, research in this area is routinely conducted with this type of data due to the difficulty of obtaining access to court decisions not appearing in official reporters (Wenner 1982; Wenner and Dutter 1988).

Another problem with the data is that they combine the decisions in asylum-related appeals of both federal district courts (which normally function as trial courts) and courts of appeal (which generally function as appellate courts). At first glance, considering all courts together may appear to be non-transitivity, a problem alluded to by Sprague (1968). However, non-transitivity only arises when district courts operate as trial courts and courts of appeals operate as appellate courts. The two types of courts thus operate in an entirely different fashion, with district courts making both factual and legal findings while appeals courts are limited to considering questions of law raised at trial. In the instant analysis, this problem does not arise because both district courts and courts of appeals in asylum-related appeals are operating as appellate courts. The normal case considered is one in which an alien sought asylum or withholding from the INS or an immigration judge, had his or her request denied, and then pursued an unsuccessful appeal to the BIA. After having no success with the BIA, the alien pursued an appeal, pursuant to federal statutes, to either a district court or a court of appeals.

This study explores the relationship between decisions on asylum-related appeals and the following independent variables: (1) the political party affiliation of the president who appointed the judge or judges involved in an appeal; (2) the level of immigrant flow into a judge's circuit; (3) the involvement of interest groups in the appeal; (4) the region of the decision maker; (5) the unemployment rate; (6) whether the alien is from a "hostile" country; and (7) whether the alien is European.

The dependent variable is outcome in asylum-related appeals to the federal district courts or courts of appeals, measured as the holding or decision of the whole court, and not the decisions of individual members. Hence, in district court cases, where only one judge sits, the outcome is the decision of the single district court judge. However, in court of appeals cases, in which three judges preside, the outcome is the decision of the whole court, not that of each individual member of the panel. Further, the dependent variable is addressed to whether the alien involved in the asylum-related appeal "won" the appeal, where a win is construed to be a judicial decision that benefits the alien.

The first independent variable, relating to partisanship, is measured as follows: high/low percentage of judges involved in an appeal who were appointed by a Democratic president. This variable has been dichotomized at its mean: 49 percent of all judges involved in the 146 appeals were appointed by a Democratic president. One complicating factor is that district court decision making is engaged in by one individual and courts of appeals determinations are arrived at by a panel of three. Hence, for the purposes of measurement, when a district court judge involved in a case was appointed by a Democratic president, 100 percent of the judges were appointed by a Democratic president. In an appeals panel, if one of the judges were appointed by a Democratic president, 33 percent of the judges involved were appointed by a Democratic president.

The involvement of interest groups in the asylum-related appeals is measured by examining each of the written decisions for the 146 appeals, which list the litigants involved in the appeals, their counsel, the interest groups involved in the case, and whether they appeared in a representative capacity or as *amicus curiae*.

High/low flow of immigrants into the judicial circuit of the judge(s) involved in an appeal is measured through an examination of whether the flow of immigrants into a circuit in 1984—the midpoint for these appeals—was high relative to the total population of the circuit (1984 Statistical Yearbook of the Immigration and Naturalization Service, U.S. Department of Justice; State and Metropolitan Area Data Book 1986, U.S. Bureau of the Census). This variable has been dichotomized at its mean of 14 percent.

For the sake of consistency with prior research on the relationship between geographic region of judges and court outcomes (Wenner and Dutter 1988), judges involved in the 146 asylum-related appeals have been grouped, by circuit, into the following geographic regions: North, consisting of the 1st, 2nd, and 3rd circuits; South, consisting of the 4th, 5th, and 6th circuits; Midwest, consisting of the 6th, 7th, and 8th circuits; and West, consisting of the 9th and 10th circuits. Although critics might charge that these judicial circuits do not correspond with natural social or economic regions (for example, Midwest circuits include both Arkansas and Tennessee), Wenner and Dutter (1988: 98) suggest that the federal judicial circuits "do reflect a grouping of states into regions that were designed to be contiguous and compact for the purposes of communication. . . . Each circuit forms a small legal culture of its own."

The Washington, D.C. circuit is excluded from the analysis of the relationship of geographic region to court outcomes, since judges in the D.C. circuit are appointed from around the United States, and one does not expect regional influences on judicial decision making to be consistent in the D.C. circuit (Wenner and Dutter 1988).

The unemployment rate is measured as follows: high/low unemployment rate for six months prior to the month in which a decision was rendered. For district courts, the unemployment rate is taken for the city in which the district court judge sits. For courts of appeals, the unemployment rate is calculated by taking the average unemployment rate for the six-month period in the three cities in which judges sit (U.S. Department of Labor 1980–87). There is some arbitrariness in measuring the unemployment rate for the six-month period before judges make decisions on appeals. Some would argue, for example, that this period is of too short a duration. Although this contention is true, some cut-off point has to be made, and there is a danger in extending the observation period to, for example, one year because one assumes in doing so that judges involved in these appeals recall what the unemployment rate was one year ago. The mean unemployment rate for the 146 appeals is 6.86; this variable has been dichotomized at its mean.

Most appeals contain information on the country of origin of the alien or aliens involved in the appeal. In order to determine whether the countries of origin of aliens are hostile to the United States, background notes published by the U.S. State Department, Bureau of Public Affairs were consulted (U.S. Department of State 1980–87. When these notes suggest that a country has a communist, socialist, or leftist form of government, this country is labeled "hostile." From the same source, it is also possible to determine whether the aliens are from Europe.

Statistical analysis consists of probit analysis because the dependent variable, whether aliens prevail in their asylum-related appeals to the federal courts, is dichotomous and there are multiple independent variables. Probit allows one to examine the relationship between multiple independent variables and a dependent variable when controlling for the effects of the other variables. Probit analysis has been employed in similar research contexts (Wenner and Dutter 1988; Segal 1984; Wall 1985).

Findings: Relationships between Federal Court Outcomes and the Independent Variables

After deletion of insignificant independent variables (unemployment rate, South, North, Midwest), Table 2.1 shows the results of probit analysis.

The equation has overall statistical significance ($p < 0.005$), and there is a fair measure of goodness of fit. The percentage predicted correctly is 71 percent.

The only statistically significant independent variables in the equation are: organizational involvement, a high percentage of Democratic presidential appointees, and high immigrant flow—the three political variables. Organizational participation is significantly related to outcome in asylum-related appeals when controlling for the effects of the other independent variables ($p < 0.005$). Organizational involvement in the appeals increases an alien's chances of success.

The partisanship variable is also significantly related to outcome when controlling for other independent variables ($p < 0.005$). The presence of judges appointed by Democratic presidents tends to increase an alien's chances of prevailing in his or her asylum-related appeal to the federal courts.

The constituency variable, high flow of immigrants into a judge or judges circuit, is statistically significant ($p < 0.005$). A high percentage of immigrants in a judge's circuit increases the probability that the decision will favor the alien or aliens involved in the appeal.

Table 2.1

Probit Estimates for Federal District Court and Court of Appeals Determinations in Asylum-Related Appeals, 1980–87

Dependent Variable: Alien Prevailed In Aslylum-Related Appeal

Mean: 42%

Variable	Maximum Likelihood Estimate (MLE)	Standard Error (SE)	MLE/SE
Constant	-1.28	0.36	-3.58 **
Organization Involved	0.67	0.25	2.66 **
Hostile State Of Origin	-0.19	0.24	-0.79
European State Of Origin	0.12	0.54	0.23
West Region	0.29	0.26	1.12
High % Dem Pres Appointees	0.64	0.23	2.78 **
High Immigrant Flow	0.65	0.37	1.77 *
-2 times LLR, with DF = 7	27.89**		
Estimated R2	0.27		
% Correctly Predicted	71.00		
N = 146			

**Significant at 0.005
*Significant at 0.05

Discussion

In sharp contrast to the view of the federal courts as apolitical, federal court outcomes in asylum-related appeals during the period of 1980–87 were significantly related to three political variables: the political party affiliations of the president who appointed the judge or judges involved in an appeal, the nature of judicial constituencies, and the involvement of interest groups in these appeals. Two contextual variables were found to be not significantly related to outcome: region and the unemployment rate. Further, the federal courts departed from the biases of the immigration bureaucracy in favor of aliens from Europe and aliens from hostile countries.

The fact that the partisanship variable is significantly related to judicial decision making coincides with the suggestion of many analysts that federal court judges do not exist in a political vacuum but are instead subject to the influence of their surrounding political environment. The link to the political environment is even greater for federal court judges than for most citizens, since they tend to be partisan activists prior to their appointment and to have held significant elective or appointive office prior to their selection. For example, most federal court judges, prior to their appointment, have held positions in state courts (most of which select judges through partisan politics), administration (their appointment to agency positions is at least partly dependent on their partisan affiliation), and elective political office (Baum 1989). Further, the partisan affiliation of federal court judges is an important criterion for judicial selection. Goldman (1975), Nagel (1961), Vines (1963), and Carp and Rowland (1983) suggest that presidents tend to appoint as judges persons from their own political parties.

Of course, one is not certain how to interpret this finding. The importance of partisanship in federal court decision making may be an indication that federal court judges, after their appointment, "stick to the party line" when making decisions in individual cases. This is not an unreasonable suggestion; given that federal court judges have had, for the most part, very partisan pasts, one does not expect that these decision makers will abandon their partisan loyalties after they have acquired the black robes of judicial office. Further, federal court judges may retain partisan loyalties due to the prospect of future promotion within the ranks of the judiciary or appointment to administrative positions. The selection of Supreme Court justices, for example, is strongly influenced by the partisan affiliation of candidates (Baum 1989), as is the selection of top-level administrators.

An alternate way to interpret the finding that federal court decision making is influenced by partisanship is to suggest that the ideology and/or background of a judge may be summed to "political party" and that what we are finding is that the ideology or background of a judge appears to influence judicial decision making.

Other aspects of the political environment that appear to be related to judicial decision making are the preferences of judicial constituents, defined as those individuals in the decision makers circuit who will be most directly affected by the decision. In the case of asylum-related appeals, the relevant constituency was identified as the immigrant population within a judge's circuit. The higher the percentage of immigrants in a judge's circuit relative to total population, the greater the probability that an alien will prevail in his or her asylum-related appeal to the federal courts. Perhaps in high immigrant-flow areas, immigrants have become well integrated into the political, economic, and cultural life of the larger community. Groups may be organized to promote the interests of immigrants, and judges who reside in these areas may be more sympathetic toward immigrants, including asylees, than judges in low immigrant-flow areas.

This finding coincides with the suggestion of analysts that judges are influenced by public opinion, since constituent preferences are nothing more than the presumed preferences of certain members of the public. Cook's (1981) analysis of federal district judges sentencing decisions in draft evasion cases found that these decisions were related to public opinion. Baum (1989) suggests, in his discussion of Supreme Court decision making, that courts are unlikely to adopt policies that fail to maintain minimum levels of social support.

It may also be that the previous political careers of federal court judges make them sensitive to public demands. Further, they may not want to jeopardize future political or judicial appointments through unpopular decisions.

Given the seeming importance of interest groups in politics in the United States generally (Schattschneider 1960; Olson 1971; Lowi 1979; McFarland 1980), it is not altogether surprising that the presence of interest groups in asylum-related appeals is significantly related to outcome, and that aliens who were either represented by an interest group or had an interest group arguing on their behalf as *amicus curiae* had an increased chance of prevailing in their appeals. In favoring aliens with organizational involvement in their appeals, federal court judges may have been acting politically. If these judges seek promotion within the judiciary or administrative appointments, they may have decided these cases in favor of aliens as a way of courting the support of the interest groups involved in the appeal. These types of interest groups often testify before congressional committees on the qualifications of prospective judicial and political appointees, and it is generally acknowledged that their testimony may be critical (Baum 1989).

Alternately, one may explain the "organizational advantage" in these appeals by arguing that organizations have superior litigation resources. Galanter (1974, 1978) and others (Dolbeare 1978; Epstein 1985; Wenner 1982; Wenner and Dutter 1988) agree that organizations, as "repeat players" in litigation, tend to win cases more often than individuals who are not repeatedly involved in litigation. Even with a private attorney, the latter do not have the advantages that accrue to organizations involved in litigation on a continuous basis. First, organizations gain experience and expertise in litigation and may have organizational resources and information that may be used to argue the merits of a case (Vose 1959; O'Connor 1980). Certain organizations, particularly public interest organizations, engage in extensive interaction with other organizations involved in similar litigation. As a result of informal exchanges of information and more formal cooperative efforts, organizations are able to maximize their effectiveness in litigation. The continuous input from these organizations may induce courts to change the governing rules to their advantage (Galanter 1974, 1978).

The second explanation is that aliens with organizational involvement in their appeals were more successful than aliens without organizational involvement due to the superior litigation resources of organizations. Since aliens were pitted against a repeat player in these appeals—the federal government—the involvement of organizations on their behalf made for a more balanced contest.

In spite of the importance economists give to economic factors, the unemployment rate was not significantly related to outcome in asylum-related appeals to the federal courts. The insignificance of this economic variable may be due to the fact that, unlike the United States' general immigration policy, which is probably influenced by economic conditions, the refugee and asylum policy areas are subject to political and humanitarian considerations, not economic ones.

Geographic region is also not significantly related to federal court outcomes in asylum-related appeals. Perhaps regional differences of decision makers become relevant only when the issues the decision makers are considering are major, conflictual issues, giving rise to ideological and regional division—issues such as abortion and race relations. On these major issues, one might expect that regional patterns will emerge among decision makers. However, the refugee and asylum policy of the United States does not fall into this category of issues, and hence should not provoke different reactions from federal court judges in different regions of the country.

Federal refugee and asylum policy is subject to political, humanitarian, and international considerations. As a result of these countervailing forces, the ensuing policy is ambiguous and conflicting, leading to vague decision rules that leave administrators and judges with a great deal of discretion. Court outcomes appear to be molded, to some extent, by political variables. The danger is that the merits of individual claims for asylum and withholding are being overlooked in asylum-related appeals as federal court judges are influenced by the partisan affiliation of appointing presidents, the preferences of their constituencies, and the lobbying of interest groups.

If it is not possible to remove political factors from the decision making of federal court judges, then the federal judiciary, like the other political branches, should be held accountable through the electoral process.

CASE STUDY 2: WHEN JUDGES ARE SHIELDED FROM POLITICAL PRESSURES

Apolitical Courts: Rape Sentencing in Montana

This analysis examines dockets of the state courts of Montana for the years 1987–89 in rape cases to determine whether sentencing decisions are related to political and legally relevant variables. Before turning to this analysis, it is helpful to review recent attempts to reform existing rape laws.

Background: Rape Reform Legislation

Critics of the criminal justice system suggest that the position of women has not been advanced by the courts, whether they appear as litigants, attorneys, or defendants in criminal cases (Crites and Hepperle 1987; Bowker 1978). They claim that sexism, or general societal discrimination against women, manifests itself in the courts, particularly in cases in which women are victims of rape or sexual assault. Historically, state rape statutes were drafted in such a way that rape convictions were rare. Spencer (1978) suggests that enforcers of rape laws (including police, prosecutors, and judges) tended to place the blame for rape on victims rather than on perpetrators. In the wake of the women's liberation movement, amendments were made in archaic statutes that generally improved the position of rape victims. For example, although rape statutes vary from state to state, many undertook to (1) redefine rape, (2) establish different degrees of rape, (3) bar evidence of the previous sexual conduct of the victim (which had often been used to discredit her testimony), (4) adopt more stringent penalties, and (5) delete requirements for corroborating evidence (Spencer 1978).

The state of Montana also joined the ranks of states that have reformed their rape laws. Amendments to Montana's Penal Code, particularly during the 1980s, redefined rape, established different degrees of rape, banned evidence of previous sexual conduct, and adopted more stringent penalties (Montana Code Annotated 1988).

In spite of apparent legislative victories that presumably facilitate convictions on rape charges, critics suggest that legal reforms have not resulted in a dramatic increase in rape convictions. Instead, Spencer (1978) argues that judges are not greatly influenced by the law but by "external forces." As an example, she cites the fact that 22 states (in 1978) allowed rapists to be sent to prison for life, and Mississippi at that time even allowed for punishment by death. In spite of these severe penalties, the willingness to prosecute and sentence rapists is based on perceptions of police, prosecutors, and judges about the victim's character.

"Good" rapes are more likely to be prosecuted than "bad" rapes, according to Spencer (1978). "Good" rapes tend to show substantial evidence of non-consent such as physical injury, the presence of weapons, breaking and entering of the premises of the victim, and no previous relationship between the rapist and the victim. "Bad" rapes tend to show no physical evidence of resistance, involve suspect victims such as prostitutes and a previous relationship between the victim and the accused (Spencer 1978). This reflects broadly based expectations that women will remain chaste and fight to the death to protect their chastity.

Bowker (1978) agrees with the foregoing, suggesting that contemporary rape laws among the states do not constitute a major departure from earlier rape laws, which were enacted when women in the United States were still considered to be the property of their husbands. She suggests that stringent standards of proof still apply in rape cases, which interfere with convictions on rape charges. Some of the reasons for these stringent burdens of proof include (1) the belief that many women fantasize about rape, (2) the view that juries are sympathetic to rape victims, and (3) the cultural legacy of sexism in the United States (Bowker 1978).

Recent reforms in state sexual assault legislation referred to above came, as the authors note, in the wake of the women's liberation movement. A 1980 study suggested that since the early 1970s, 32 states have instituted comprehensive reform of their rape laws (Lawson 1984). Many of the reforms, lobbied for by public interest organizations such as the National Organization for Women (NOW), are similar in several essential details. Traditional penal code provisions unduly limited their definitions of rape. One example is the Illinois Criminal Code of 1961, which stated: "A male person of the age of 14 years and upwards who has sexual intercourse with a female, not his wife, by force and against her will, commits rape."

New sexual assault statutes have eliminated many of the requirements of earlier rape laws. An example is the Illinois Criminal Sexual Assault Act of 1984, which eliminated the gender stipulation, the age requirement, the marital exemption (for Class X offenses), and replaced the crime of rape with four classes of sex offenses. The Illinois law divides sex crimes into criminal sexual assault and criminal sexual abuse. Sexual assault includes forcible sexual penetration, both heterosexual and homosexual. Sexual abuse is forcible sexual conduct that does not include intercourse (Lawson 1984). The new sex crime statute takes into account a new understanding of deviate sexual behavior.

According to Lawson (1984), the primary objective of the new sex crime legislation in Illinois was to increase convictions. Past laws tended to impair prosecution efforts because prosecutors had to establish that the victim did not consent and the rape was forcible. Also, many rape laws contained severe penalties (such as life imprisonment) that interfered with the willingness of juries to convict.

A "Report of the Overcrowding Task Force," completed in November 1988 by the Department of Corrections of the State of Vermont (Department of Corrections 1988), indicates that this goal has been partially achieved. Specifically, the task force report suggests that most of the increase in the felony population within Vermont correctional facilities is due to an increase in the number of sex offenders. The single category of sex offender accounts for more than 50 percent of the increase in prison population from 1983 to 1987. The task force compares its findings with the reports of similar task forces in 15 other states and finds that other states also have increasing prison populations, mostly due to increases in the sex offender classification. According to its survey, sex offenders constitute 16.6 percent of the total prison population growth nationally. The study links the increase in sex offenders in Vermont to reform legislation passed by state legislators.

An interesting note with respect to the findings of the Vermont Department of Corrections Task Force is that in spite of the fact that the prison population has grown in part due to an increase in sex offenders, state court judges still granted probation in 1987 to 68.4 percent of all sex crime felons in four counties in that state (Department of Corrections 1988).

By 1990, most states had abandoned previous rape statutes in favor of "sexual assault" statutes that, like the Illinois act, tend to eliminate some of the inequities in previous rape laws. These penal code reforms appear to have been instigated in large part by public interest organizations like NOW. For example, in her discussion of reform legislation introduced in Illinois, Lawson (1984) suggests that the original bill (H.B. 606) was drafted by NOW and the Illinois Coalition of Women Against Rape. This group later met with the Rape Study Committee of the Illinois House of Representatives to draft the bill, which was subsequently introduced, and brought in 20 criminal law experts to testify during hearings. Later amendments to the legislation were made in consultation with members of the women's groups (Lawson 1984). Hence, women's rights organizations play a major role in shaping contemporary sexual assault legislation.

As mentioned, Montana also adopted rape reform laws, partially due to intense lobbying from women's groups. The following examines the extent to which state court judges have served to implement rape reform laws in their rape-sentencing decisions. It further examines the extent to which these decisions are related to political and legally relevant variables.

Hypotheses

In contrast to the traditional model of the judiciary as a passive interpreter of the law, judges examined in this analysis were not unduly restrained in their decision making by the law, due to the vagueness of standards they were called on to interpret. In rape cases arising under section 45-5-503 of the Montana Criminal Code (sexual intercourse without consent), the courts were concerned with whether the perpetrator of the crime was a danger to society, thus justifying incarceration, or whether the defendant could be safely released. There are few standards in state statutes that bind judges to employ certain criteria in their decision making. For example, trial courts in Montana, referred to as district courts, are given virtually no statutory direction in terms of both the length of sentences and in their decision to suspend or defer sentences. A suspended sentence involves the rather important decision to release an individual who has been found guilty of a crime (Newman and Anderson 1989). A deferred sentence is identical, for all practical purposes, to a suspended sentence. For the sake of simplicity, both suspended and deferred sentences will be referred to as "release decisions." In spite of the importance of these decisions, Montana gives only vague instruction to its district judges: One convicted of violating section 45-5-503 is subject to a minimum term of imprisonment of two years and a maximum of 20. However, the maximum may be increased to 40 years if the victim is under sixteen years of age and there are three or more years separating the ages of the victim and the perpetrator.

Many experts have commented on the fact that there are generally few guidelines given to judges in these cases and on the apparent arbitrariness of sentencing decisions made by judges (Frankel 1973; O'Leary, Gottfredson, and Gelman 1975; Griswold 1987) Even in the absence of specific state statutes, state court judges would have more direction in their sentencing decisions if they had a clear idea of the underlying policy objectives in this area. However, as noted by Frankel (1973) and others (Morris 1981; Allen 1981; Robinson and Smith 1981; Rothman 1981), the goals of criminal justice systems, of which sentencing is a part, have not been clearly articulated.

Another factor that contributes to the great discretion judges wield in sentencing decisions is that most convictions result from a guilty plea, rather than from a trial. For example, in a sample of 71 district court sentencing decisions entered during the period 1980–87 in rape cases pursuant to section 45-5-503 of the Montana Criminal Code (referred to in the statute as "sexual intercourse without consent"), three-quarters of the convictions resulted from a guilty plea. Trials were held in only 25 percent of the cases, prior to sentencing by judges. This suggests that judges are often unfamiliar with the important facts of a case.

Nevertheless, in the absence of both law (sentencing guidelines) and essential facts (relating to criminal defendants), judges routinely engage in sentencing decisions (Frankel 1973).

It should come as no surprise, given the vagueness of the underlying standards for sentencing, that judicial decisions have been attacked as arbitrary and, in some cases, biased.

As a result of their discretion, courts may be able to substitute their own goals for statutory goals. One thus anticipates that state court outcomes may be related to extraneous (or non-legal) variables. The following discussion reviews some extraneous independent variables drawn from public law research that have been found to be related to judicial decision making.

Political Variables

Political variables may be significantly related to state court sentencing decisions in sexual assault cases. This suggestion may seem anomalous, given that courts are generally viewed as immune to political influences because their members have been socialized into objectivity. Many states have adopted the federal standards for selection of judges, namely appointment, with the goal of ensuring that state court judges are immune to political pressures. In Montana, for example, most state court judges are selected through non-partisan elections. Over one half (52 percent) of the judges who were involved in sentencing defendants for violations of 45-5-503 (in this analysis) were elected. When a vacancy occurs, a Judicial Nomination Commission submits the names of three to five nominees to the governor. Trial court judges (referred to as district court judges) are selected from this list by the governor; judicial appointees must, in turn, be confirmed by the Senate. The Judicial Nomination Commission has seven members: Four are appointed by the governor, two are attorneys appointed by the Supreme Court of Montana, and one is a district judge elected by district court judges from around the state. No member of the commission may be nominated for a judicial position during his tenure on the commission and for four years following the end of his term (State of Montana Supreme Court 1988).

However, in the same way that courts have been shown to engage in policy making and not merely legal interpretation, many analysts concede that judicial decision making, both at state and federal levels, is often linked to political factors. Judges do not operate in a vacuum and may be influenced by their environment, including their political environment.

Political Party. If judges are influenced by political variables, perhaps state court judges are influenced in their decision making by their political party affiliation (Baum 1989; Goldman 1975; Nagel 1961; Vines 1963; Yarnold 1990a, 1991b; Carp and Rowland 1983). Judges who are either affiliated with the Democratic Party or whose court sits in a Democratic county may be more lenient in their sentencing of convicted rapists than Republican judges, due to the general commitment of the Democratic Party to social and economic "underdogs," including criminal defendants (Cummings and Wise 1985).

Appointed or Elected Judges. The extent to which political influences affect judicial decision making may be determined to some extent by the judicial selection process. If judges are selected through partisan elections, they may be more subject to partisan effects than are judges who are either appointed or chosen in non-partisan elections.

Judicial Constituencies and Public Opinion. Another political variable that may influence state court judges is public opinion (Cook 1981; Baum 1989), or the preferences of "judicial constituents" (Yarnold 1990a, 1991b).

In evaluating the link between policy making and constituency preferences, one must address the question of which constituency of the decision maker might be most directly affected by the decision in question (Yarnold 1990a, 1991b). In rape cases, the constituency most likely to be affected by sentencing decisions is women. The presence of a politically powerful female constituency in a judge's county may influence judicial sentencing in rape cases.

One way to assess the political clout of women in counties is to measure the percentage of county executive offices held by women. A hypothesis is that trial court judges from counties with a high percentage of female executives will more likely impose longer sentences in rape cases than will judges in counties with a low percentage of female executives.

Variables Drawn from Criminal Justice

Analysts within the area of criminal justice are in fundamental agreement with public law researches in one key respect: their suggestion that judges have great discretion in their decision making, particularly in sentencing decisions, and that what contributes to this discretion is the absence of unambiguous laws. At this point, however, the focus of the two disciplines often diverges. Public law specialists tend to focus on political and environmental explanations of judicial decision making. They may overlook important variables raised by criminal justice analysts when the subject of research is judicial decisions in the criminal law area.

One suggestion, for example, made by Dawson (1969) and Griswold (1987) is that judges tend to penalize criminal defendants who choose to go to trial instead of pleading guilty (Miethe 1987). Thus, a competing hypothesis to the political variables is that sentencing decisions are significantly related to whether a criminal defendant requests a trial.

A second fact is the age of a judge who renders a decision (Myers 1988). Perhaps older judges, in accordance with stereotypes, give the most severe sentences to convicted rapists. A related issue is whether female judges exhibit more or less tolerance toward rapists in their sentencing decisions than male judges (Schur 1971; Nagel and Hagan 1983).

Another possibility is that sentencing decisions are related to the per capita crime rate (Hagan 1987). Trial court judges may give less severe sentences to individuals convicted of rape in counties plagued by high crime rates since detention facilities in these areas may be overcrowded.

Also mentioned in sentencing studies is the question of whether a defendant is charged with multiple law violations. It is asserted that multiple charges against a defendant tend to increase the severity of sentencing (Miethe 1987; Unnever and Hembroff 1988).

Data and Methods

Data for this analysis consist of sentencing decisions of district courts in Montana for the years 1987–89, in cases in which a defendant has been found guilty (either through a guilty plea or trial) of rape (statutorily labeled "sexual intercourse without consent").

One major criminal statute is involved in this analysis: section 45-5-503 of the Montana Criminal Code. Data for this analysis consist of the 1987–89 dockets of all district court cases that were filed under this section. There are 36 district judges in the state, most of whom are elected in non-partisan elections for six-year terms. If a vacancy occurs, appointment is made by the governor from a list of nominees provided by an independent judicial nomination commission. There is no intermediate appellate court in the state; appeals from decision of district court judges are heard by the Supreme Court of Montana. District court judges preside over courts in each of the 56 counties within the state. During the period of 1987–89, 71 cases arose under section 45-5-503; these cases provide the data for this analysis.

The dependent variable is the length of the sentence given to a convicted rapist, measured in months.

It is not possible to measure directly the first independent variable, the partisan affiliation of district court judges. However, a surrogate measure of this is the percentage of voters in the county in which a decision is rendered which voted for the Democratic candidate in the 1984 presidential election; this information is available in the *County and City Data Book 1988* (U.S. Bureau of Census 1988).

The official court dockets for sentencing decisions of district courts in section 45-5-503 cases (1987–89) provide information on the identity of the judges involved in these cases. The Administrative Office of the Montana Supreme Court also provided information on whether presiding judges were elected or appointed, the second independent variable.

To assess the strength of women as a judicial constituency, a measure was taken of the percentage in 1985 of county executive officials in a judge's county (or more precisely, in the county in which the presiding court is located) who were female. The source for this data is *The Municipal Yearbook 1989* (International City Management Association 1989). County executive officials may include the board chairman, an appointed administrator, a clerk to the governing board, the chief financial officer, the personnel director, and the chief law enforcement official. Not all counties had all of these executive positions.

Table 2.2
Regression Estimates for State Court Sentencing Decisions in Rape Cases,
1987–89

Dependent Variable: Length Of Sentence (In Months)

Variable	Coefficient	Standard Error	Standard Coef	Tol. Lvl.	T	P (2-Tail)
Constant	-442.10	292.60	0.00	--	-1.51	0.14
Plea	18.10	74.00	0.00	0.86	0.24	0.81
Crime	0.00	0.00	0.30	0.75	2.22	0.03 *
Multichrg	169.30	65.60	0.30	0.82	2.58	0.01 *
Democ84	0.80	5.40	0.00	0.54	0.15	0.88
Govwomen	-0.70	2.40	-0.00	0.48	-0.29	0.77
Appointmnt	-5.20	63.90	-0.00	0.85	-0.08	0.94
AgeJ89	5.60	3.60	0.20	0.77	1.57	0.12
JFemale	7.40	158.30	0.00	0.79	0.05	0.96

N = 65
Multiple R = 0.43   Adjusted Squared Multiple R = 0.07
Squared Multiple R = 0.19   Standard Error Of Estimate: 237.85
F = 1.6   DF = 8   P = 0.14
*Significant at 0.05

The fourth variable, whether the conviction results from a guilty plea, is obtained from official court dockets.

The fifth variable, per capita crime rate (serious crimes) of the county in which the court is located, is drawn from the *County and City Data Book 1988* (U.S. Bureau of Census 1988). The crime rates listed are for 1985, which is not the same as the years in which sentencing decisions were made. Of course, county crime rates may have increased since that time. This is probably not an obstacle, since the analysis is concerned with relative crime rates between counties, which in all likelihood have not changed in the period between 1985 and 1987–89.

The official court dockets list whether the defendant, charged with violating section 45-5-503, has also been charged with the commission of other offenses. Information provided by the Administrative Office of the Montana Supreme Court yields the age and gender of district court judges.

Statistical analysis consists of regression analysis because the dependent variable, length of sentence, is continuous and there are multiple independent variables. Regression analysis allows one to examine the relationship between multiple independent variables and a dependent variable when controlling for the other variables. The results of this analysis are shown in Table 2.2.

The only statistically significant independent variables are crime rate ($p = 0.03$) and multiple charges against a defendant ($p = 0.01$), two legally relevant variables. The overall equation lacks statistical significance ($p = 0.14$). However,

Table 2.3
Regression Estimates for State Court Sentencing Decisions in Rape Cases, 1987–89

Dependent Variable: Length Of Sentence (In Months)

Variable	Coefficient	Standard Error	Standard Coef	Tol. Lvl.	T	P (2-Tail)
Constant	-411.80	218.57	0.00	--	-1.88	0.06
Crime	0.00	0.02	0.30	0.94	2.69	0.01 *
Multichrg	168.50	58.90	0.30	0.94	2.86	0.01 *
AgeJ89	5.20	3.16	0.20	0.91	1.65	0.10

N = 65
Multiple R = 0.43   Adjusted Squared Multiple R = 0.14
Squared Multiple R = 0.18   Standard Error Of Estimate: 228.20
F = 4.60   DF = 3   P = 0.01
*Significant at 0.05

its significance increases (p = 0.01) when most of the insignificant variables are eliminated, as seen in Table 2.3.

Discussion

Although Montana was among those states that, in enacting new rape re-form legislation, appeared to be advancing the interests of women and catering to vocal women's groups, state court judges were not generally committed to implementing these laws during the period 1987–89. Although section 45-5-503 of the Montana Criminal Code provides for a minimum penalty of two years and a maximum penalty of twenty years (forty years if the victim is under sixteen and there is a three-year or more range between the ages of the offender and victim), 41 percent of those convicted of this crime were sentenced to less than two years. Further, almost one-quarter (24 percent of those convicted were released (their sentences were often deferred or suspended) with no period of confinement ordered.

The only variables that are significantly related to court outcomes in these cases are legally relevant ones: multiple charges against a defendant and the crime rate in the county in which a defendant is tried. Somewhat surprising is the fact that whether a defendant pleaded guilty or went to trial did not affect these sentencing decisions. However, when defendants were charged with multiple law violations, state court judges in Montana tended to impose longer sentences. It is reasonable that the full weight of the law was thus imposed on the most dangerous criminal offenders.

Somewhat less justifiable, however, is the fact that criminals who had the misfortune of being tried in counties with high crime rates tended to receive harsher sentences than did those in low crime rate counties. Higher crime rates are generally associated with urban areas (Engel 1985; Lineberry and Sharkansky 1978). Although precise data is not available, it may be that those who received the most severe sentences are members of the urban underclass, consisting of the poor, the uneducated, and racial and ethnic minorities.

Contrary to predictions, the state courts of Montana were not influenced in their rape-sentencing decisions during the period 1987–89 by three "political" variables: the extent to which the county in which a case is heard is Democratic, the political clout of women in the county in which a case is tried, and whether the judge who sentenced a defendant was appointed or elected.

One explanation for this finding is that the measures chosen for the political variables are unsound. For example, to measure the importance of women as a judicial constituency in counties in which sentencing decisions were made, the analysis surveyed the percentage of county officials who are women. Although a better measure of the political clout of women in counties may be their educational levels, this information is not available (which is somewhat surprising, given the profuse amount of educational data that are available). The measure chosen does indicate to some extent whether women are active in the political life of their counties.

It appears that political factors were not significant in rape-sentencing decisions by Montana state courts from 1987 to 1989. How does one reconcile this finding with previous studies that link judicial outcomes to political variables?

One possibility is that the sentencing decisions of the state courts of Montana are an aberration and thus shed no light on whether sentencing decisions are generally subject to political influences. It may be that the state of Montana has a "traditionalistic" political culture in which popular participation in politics is low and the public defers to a political and economic elite (Elazar 1972). Hence, the general public, including women, may be politically inactive. For the same reason, partisanship is not likely to be an important factor.

However, Elazar (1972) categorized Montana as a "moralistic-traditionalistic" state in which public participation in politics tends to be high, and individuals become involved in politics first, for the "public good," and only secondly for private gain. Hence, the suggestion that Montana judges, unlike other judges, are immune to political pressure due to the nature of the underlying political culture is unfounded.

The results of this analysis may not be explained away by the assertion that the decisions of Montana courts in rape sentencing represent an aberration. Instead, they may be fairly representative of state court outcomes in rape cases in states with similar political systems.

It was also predicted that the partisanship variable (the percentage of county that voted Democratic in the 1984 presidential election) would be significantly related to judicial sentencing decisions. This prediction is based on three assumptions: that judges are generally subject to the influence of their political environments; that Democratic judges tend to deal less harshly with criminals than Republicans; and that judges from heavily Democratic regions will issue lenient

sentences in rape cases either (1) because they are members of the Democratic
Party or (2) to avoid alienating county residents who are Democratic Party
members.

Some analysts suggest that the link to the political environment is even greater
for judges than for most citizens because judges tend to be partisan activists
prior to their appointment or election and to have held significant elective or
appointive office prior to their selection (Baum 1989). Further, the partisan
affiliation of both state and federal court judges is an important criterion for
judicial selection because political parties tend to look for partisan loyalists when
slating candidates for judgeships (Goldman 1975; Nagel 1961; Vines 1963; Carp
and Rowland 1983).

It was earlier argued (Yarnold 1990a, 1991b) that after their appointment or
election, judges follow the party line when making decisions in individual cases.
This is not unreasonable, given that judges have had, for the most part, very
partisan pasts. One does not anticipate that they will abandon their partisan
loyalties after acquiring judicial office. Judges may believe they need the support
of their parties to get re-elected. Further, judges may retain partisan loyalties in
the hope of future promotion within the ranks of the judiciary or appointment to
other prominent positions.

This last point seems to have some support in the context of district court
judges in Montana. Only one or two years after entering the orders in the cases
involved in this analysis, several trial court judges had advanced in their careers.
Two were promoted to the Supreme Court of Montana, one was assigned to be
chief water court judge, and another had become a U.S. magistrate.

Based on the foregoing, one anticipates that state court judges, in their
sentencing decisions in rape cases, are influenced by their partisanship (or
the partisanship of the county in which their court resides). However, an
intervening variable is the reform character of the judicial selection process
in Montana. Judges are either elected in non-partisan elections or, if a vacancy
occurs, appointed by the governor from a list of three nominees provided by an
independent judicial nomination commission. Four members of this commission
are appointed by the governor, two are attorneys appointed by the Montana
Supreme Court, and one is a district court judge elected by district court judges
from around the state. Commission members serve a four-year term and are
not eligible for nomination to the judiciary for the duration of their term and
for four years thereafter (State of Montana Supreme Court 1988).

Hence, the ability of governors to appoint as judges members of their own
political party is blocked by the judicial nomination commission. Similarly, the
ability of voters to elect judges on the basis of their partisan affiliations is
blocked by the non-partisan character of judicial elections.

Thus, the reform character of the judicial selection process in Montana, and
particularly its emphasis on the non-partisan selection of judges, appears to have
the effect of freeing judges from partisan influences in their sentencing decisions
in rape cases. In accordance with this suggestion, the fact that a district court

judge was appointed, rather than elected, did not affect sentencing decisions, which is to be expected since both judicial elections and appointments in Montana are non-partisan.

It was also posited that other aspects of the political environment may be related to judicial decision making in rape cases, such as the preferences of judicial constituents, or those individuals in a district judge's county who will be most directly affected by the decision. In the context of sentencing in rape cases, the relevant constituency was identified as politically powerful women within a judge's county. It was predicted that a high percentage of women in county executive offices in the county in which a court sits would lead judges in that county to give harsh sentences to those convicted of rape. Where women are well represented in county governance, women as a group may be well integrated into the political and economic life of the county. Local groups may be organized to promote the interests of women, and national women's rights organizations may have affiliates in the county. Judges who hold court in these areas may be more sympathetic toward women than judges in counties where women are not as politically active. Even if not sympathetic toward women, judges may mete out harsh sentences in rape cases for the purpose of courting this important judicial constituency.

This prediction coincides with the suggestion that judges are influenced by public opinion, since constituent preferences are simply the presumed preferences of certain members of the public. It may be that the previous political careers of state court judges make them sensitive to public demands. Further, they may not want to jeopardize future political or judicial positions through unpopular decisions.

Although the above seems reasonable, once again a political variable, the political clout of women within counties in which decisions were rendered, has been shown in this analysis to be unrelated to sentencing decisions in rape cases (1987–89) by the state courts of Montana. How does one explain this apparent contradiction of earlier analyses that suggest judges are influenced by both judicial constituencies and public opinion?

The conflicting results may be reconciled by reference to an evaluation of congressional voting by Miller and Stokes (1963), who suggest that the public generally has little information on specific policy issues and hence lacks preferences on most policy issues. Building on this concept, Page et al. (1984: 753) suggest that congressional members tend to be influenced by constituent preferences only when the issues involved are "institutionalized in party cleavages and linked to broad ideology among the public, where opinions are fairly firmly held and information about congressmen is easily obtainable."

Issues may be divided into two categories: those that are major, publicized, and on which constituents have preferences that bind policy makers, and those that are minor, unpublicized, and on which constituents have no preferences that serve to restrict policy makers. To the extent that judges are policy makers, they may only be subject to the influence of their judicial constituencies or public opinion when the issues they are dealing with are major, publicized issues.

Hence, it may be that Montana state court judges did not respond in rape-sentencing decisions to their judicial constituencies (politically powerful women in county executive positions) because the decisions in these cases are not major or regularly publicized by the media. Even when the media covers a particularly egregious sentencing decision in rape cases (such as setting no term of imprisonment for a repeat offender), adverse publicity is short-lived, and generally the public memory is short. By the time that a district court judge faces re-election, it is probable that neither the public nor the press will recall what appears to be only a sporadic abuse of judicial discretion.

While judicial sentencing in rape cases does not appear to be a major issue on which constituency preferences must be taken into account, rape and, more generally, sexual assault issues do appear to be major issues when they are considered by state legislatures. As mentioned, many states, including Montana, adopted reform legislation in sex crimes at the behest of women's rights organizations, which fought legislative battles in state capitals across the country; these battles were regularly covered by the media. In state legislatures that dealt with rape and sexual assault issues, politically powerful women's organizations were thus an important political constituency.

In contrast, in this analysis, women's organizations were not involved in court proceedings that handed down sentences to those convicted of rape. There was no network of interest groups that served a watchdog function in these cases. The fact that there was no interest group involvement in these proceedings served to further insulate state court judges from political influences.

Political factors did not appear to affect state court sentencing decisions in rape cases during the period 1987–89 because: (1) sentencing decisions are not major, publicized issues; (2) the selection of state court judges (both through appointment and election) is non-partisan; and (3) interest groups were not involved in rape sentencing cases.

CASE STUDY THREE: COURTS AND FOREIGN NATIONALS

Ethnic Politics in U.S. Courts: U.S. District Court Outcomes in International Extradition Cases 1932–90

International extradition is the practice by which a fugitive is delivered from the country to which he has fled to the country that seeks his return for violations of its criminal law (Bassiouni 1983). The duty to extradite is usually based on the existence of an extradition treaty between the two states.

U.S. extradition proceedings are initiated when the agent of another country requests extradition from the U.S. State Department. Acting for the requesting country, the U.S. Attorney's Office within the Department of Justice then files an extradition request with a U.S. district court.

After the extradition request is filed, the U.S. attorney requests that the district court issue an arrest warrant for the individual whose extradition is sought, referred to as the "relator." A judge or magistrate then issues a warrant for the relator's arrest (Hall 1987). After arrest, the relator is entitled to a hearing on the question of bail (Bassiouni 1983).

Following the bail determination, a "probable cause" hearing is conducted pursuant to Title 18, Section 3184 (section 5). The purpose of the probable cause hearing is not to determine the guilt or innocence of the relator but to determine whether the evidence of criminality is sufficient to sustain charges against the respondent under the provisions of an applicable treaty (*Re Extradition of Prushinowski*, 574 F.Supp. 1439 (E.D. N.C. 1983)).

If the court grants extradition, a certificate of extraditability is sent to the U.S. State Department, which issues the final extradition order (Bassiouni 1983). However, the secretary of state (and the president) has the discretion to refuse to extradite an individual for any reason, such as concern over deficiencies in the judicial process of the requesting state (*Plaster v. United States*, 720 F.2d 340 (4th Cir. 1983); *Escobedo v. United States*, 623 F.2d 1098 (5th Cir. 1980)).

The only collateral attack on a finding of extraditability is a writ of *habeas corpus*, filed with a federal district court (*Caplan v. Vokes*, 649 F.2d 1336 (9th Cir. 1981); *United States v. Wiebe*, 733 F.2d 549 (8th Cir. 1984)). If this is denied, relators may then appeal to U.S. courts of appeals; beyond this, they may file petitions for writs of *certiorari* with the U.S. Supreme Court (28 U.S.C. Sections 2241 and 2101 (1976)).

Hypotheses

When dealing with cases that touch on other policy areas, such as environmental policy (Wenner 1982; Wenner and Dutter 1988), and U.S. policy relating to refugees and asylees (Yarnold 1990a, 1991b), federal court judges appear not to be greatly constrained in their decision making by the law. A major reason for this is that the law is typically vague (Baum 1989). Hence, it is argued that judges wield a great deal of discretion in their decision making and may be influenced by non-legal variables.

Legal standards are quite vague in extradition proceedings presided over by U.S. federal courts. Kester (1988: 1442) claims:

The substantive standards and even some of the procedures by which United States courts deal with extradition matters are scarcely spelled out by statute or in the hundred or so extradition treaties that the United States has entered into with other countries.

Case law is growing, but much of it is based on "antiquated" U.S. Supreme Court decisions (Kester 1988). Adding to the shortage of clear legal guidelines is the fact that extradition law is set forth in over 100 extradition treaties that the United States has entered into with other states (Hall 1987; Kester 1988). The status of extradition proceedings is unclear;

they are referred to as "hybrid" proceedings because they are neither criminal nor civil. Critics suggest extradition proceedings are *sui generis*, leaving judges free to improvise (Kester 1988).

Data were collected on decisions of U.S. district court judges in extradition cases (pursuant to 18 U.S.C. 3184 through 3190) included in the *Federal Supplement* since its first publication in 1933. All 86 extradition cases that appear in volumes 1 through 732 of the *Federal Supplement*, a period of approximately six decades (from October 1932 to May 14, 1990) have been included.

On the assumption that federal court judges are subject to the influence of non-legal variables, the following variables are examined in extradition cases:

Political Variables

Based on prior analysis that finds a link between judicial outcomes and political variables (Baum 1989; Yarnold 1990a, 1991b; Wenner 1982; Wenner and Dutter 1988; Cook 1981), the following political variables were examined: whether the state within which a judge is located is a high immigrant-flow area; and the partisan affiliation of the judge involved in the case or the partisan affiliation of the president who appointed the judge (sources of background data on judges: Judicial Conference 1983; Dornette and Cross 1986).

Federal court outcomes in asylum-related appeals indicated that judges from states that had a high flow of immigrants across their borders tended to decide cases in favor of aliens (Yarnold 1990a, 1991b). I argued that judges were responding to an important judicial constituency—the immigrants within their states.

One does not expect that the U.S. public generally is greatly concerned with judicial outcomes in extradition cases. However, federal court decisions in extradition cases may be of great importance to immigrants. Hence, the relevant judicial constituency in these cases may be the immigrant population within a judge's state.

Many suggest that judicial outcomes are linked to the partisan affiliation of judges or the partisan affiliations of their appointing presidents (Baum 1989; Goldman 1975; Nagel 1961; Vines 1963; Carp and Rowland 1983; Yarnold 1990a, 1991b). The extradition cases are examined to determine whether outcomes are related to the partisan affiliations of judges and their appointing presidents.

These cases are not coded on another political variable, the involvement of interest groups in litigation, because interest groups were not involved in these cases. However, some of the relators were members of a group on whose behalf they committed the crime in question. Two organizations that surface in these cases are the Irish Republican Army (IRA) and the Palestine Liberation Organization (PLO). This analysis considers whether litigants were helped or impaired in these extradition cases by their membership in these groups. Hence, a third political variable is whether the relator is a member of an organization on whose behalf he or she committed the crime in question. The analysis also examines the specific organizational affiliations of relators to determine whether membership in one confers more benefit than membership in another.

Federal court judges may also tend to grant extradition when the state seeking extradition enjoys good diplomatic relations with the United States. Farrell (1985: 7) suggests that historically, "hostile powers usually gave refuge to each other's fugitives." States seeking extradition are divided into two groups: those with communist, socialist, or leftist forms of government, and thus "hostile" to the United States, and those without such forms of government and thus "non-hostile" to the United States. Data on the communist, socialist, or leftist governments of states were gathered from "Background Notes" issued by the U.S. State Department's Bureau of Public Affairs (U.S. Department of State 1930–90). The fourth political variable is whether the requesting state is hostile to the United States.

Contextual Variables

Analysts have also taken the position that judicial decisions are linked to the geographic region of courts (Richardson and Vines 1978; Wenner 1982; Wenner and Dutter 1988; Carp and Rowland 1983; Cook 1981). This variable is included as a contextual variable.

Facts

Federal court outcomes in extradition cases may also be linked to the important facts of a case (Segal 1985; Gibson 1977; Dudley 1989; Gryski et al 1986; Haire and Songer 1990). Two facts are examined in extradition cases: whether the crime for which extradition is sought is an international crime or a state crime; and whether the relator raised the political offense exception to extradition.

The dependent variable is whether the relator won; a "win" is a judicial decision that benefits the relator. Since the dependent variable is dichotomous and there are multiple independent variables (also dichotomous), probit analysis has been performed. Probit analysis has been successfully performed in similar research contexts (Segal 1984; Wall 1985; Wenner and Dutter 1988; Yarnold 1990a, 1991b).

Findings

Table 2.4 contains the results of a probit analysis of federal district court extradition cases reported in *Federal Supplements* from 1932 to 1990. This equation lists all of the independent variables, with the exception of "IRA" (that is, whether the relator is linked to the Irish Republican Army) and "PLO" (whether the relator is linked to the Palestine Liberation Organization). The variable that has been included is "External Organization," or whether the relator is linked to an external organization on whose behalf the crime was committed. Table 2.5 includes "IRA" and "PLO" and excludes "External Organization."

The only statistically significant independent variable in the two equations is "link to IRA," or the fact that a relator committed the crime on behalf of the

Table 2.4
Probit Estimates for Federal District Court Determinations in Extradition Cases,
1932–90

Dependent Variable: Whether Relator (Individual Subject To
Extradition) Prevailed

Mean: 26%

Variable	Maximum Likelihood Estimate (MLE)	Standard Error (SE)	MLE/SE
Constant	4.60	0.79	5.78 **
High Immigration Flow	0.01	0.38	0.01
Democratic Judge	-0.10	0.36	-0.29
External Organization	1.20	0.77	1.56
Requesting State Hostile	4.14	3.79	1.09
Court In North	-0.37	0.78	-0.48
Court In Midwest	-0.81	0.97	-0.83
Court In West	0.09	0.84	0.11
Court In South	0.27	1.10	0.25
International Crime	-5.28	5.10	-1.04
Political Offense Raised	-1.06	0.78	-1.36

Chi-Square = 14.9   DF = 20   P = 0.78
N = 86
**Significant at 0.005

IRA (p < .05). The fact that a relator is linked to the IRA substantially increases the likelihood that the relator will prevail in extradition proceedings in the U.S. federal courts.

The other political variables are not significantly linked to outcome. The variable of external organization is not significant. The important factor in these cases is not whether the relator is linked to an external group but the identity of the organization and whether it has an organized, supportive ethnic group in the United States. Hence, relators linked to the PLO were damaged by this association. The average success rate for all relators in extradition cases was 26 percent; those linked to the IRA prevailed in 67 percent of the cases (n = 3), while relators linked to the PLO had a 0 percent success rate (n = 2).

The partisan affiliation of judges is not significantly related to outcome. Relators were less likely to prevail in these cases when the presiding judge was a member of the Democratic Party or appointed by a Democratic President. The constituency variable, high flow of immigrants into a judge's state relative to the population of that state, is also not significantly related to outcome.

Federal court judges deciding extradition cases favored relators from hostile states of origin, though not at a statistically significant level. Judges may

Table 2.5

Probit Estimates for Federal District Court Determinations in Extradition Cases, 1932–90

Dependent Variable: Whether Relator (Individual Subject To
Extradition) Prevailed

Mean: 26%

Variable	Maximum Likelihood Estimate (MLE)	Standard Error (SE)	MLE/SE	
Constant	4.59	0.79	5.78	**
High Immigration Flow	0.01	0.38	0.01	
Democratic Judge	-0.09	0.36	-0.26	
Link To IRA	1.48	0.84	1.76	*
Link To PLO	-2.24	17.89	-0.12	
Requesting State Hostile	3.90	3.85	1.01	
Court In North	-0.40	0.78	-0.51	
Court In Midwest	-0.73	0.97	-0.76	
Court In West	0.21	1.09	0.19	
Court In South	0.09	0.84	0.10	
International Crime	-5.30	5.18	-1.02	
Political Offense Raised	-0.76	0.75	-1.02	

Chi-Square = 16.35   DF = 20   P = 0.70

N = 86

**Significant at 0.005

*Significant at 0.05

have been aware that diplomatic relations would not be impaired by denying extradition requests from states with communist, socialist, or leftist forms of government. Hence, these decisions exhibit some latitude when relators are from hostile states.

Geographic region is not significantly related to outcome in extradition cases, which coincides with my earlier suggestion that region may be important only when the issues that courts consider are major, conflictual ones such as abortion and race relations (Yarnold 1991b). Relators were most likely to win in courts in the West, followed closely by courts in the South. Relators were at a disadvantage when their cases were presided over by judges in the North and the Midwest.

Two facts were not significantly related to outcome: whether the relator was sought for committing an international crime and whether the relator raised the political offense exception to extradition. Relators were more likely to lose in an extradition proceeding if the crime for which they were charged was an international one. Also, relators were seemingly penalized for raising the political offense exception to extradition. Those who did tended to have below-average success rates in extradition cases.

Discussion

Federal court outcomes in extradition cases appear to be related to political factors. This finding supports earlier analyses, which discovered that federal court judges are not unduly constrained by the law and facts of a case, but wield a great deal of discretion in their decision making (Frank 1978; Baum 1989).

It was suggested earlier that extradition law is quite unclear since it is set forth in over 100 extradition treaties that the United States has entered into with other states (Hall 1987; Kester 1988). It is also uncertain whether extradition proceedings are civil or criminal. One critic argues that because federal court judges are not bound by specific legal guidelines, they simply improvise in extradition cases (Kester 1988).

The facts of extradition cases do not bind federal court judges. Two critical facts in extradition cases—whether the crime for which extradition is sought is an international crime and whether the relator raises the political offense exception to extradition—are not significantly related to outcome.

Instead of applying the law to the facts of a case, federal court judges were seemingly influenced in their decision making in extradition cases by political factors.

The question arises as to why federal court judges, who are in the rather privileged position of having lifetime appointments, should be subject to political influences. In strict constitutional jurisprudence, the federal courts reside in a uniquely apolitical branch, which is one of the primary arguments in support of their power to check the excesses of the other, political branches.

It was earlier argued that "the link to the political environment is even greater for federal court judges than for most citizens" (Yarnold 1991b). One reason for the politization of the federal judiciary is that federal court judges are "political activists" in U.S. politics. As Baum (1989) suggests, federal court judges have often, prior to their appointment, held positions as state court judges and administrators. Many have also held elective political office. Hence, they have been conditioned, even after their appointment to the federal courts, to serve as political actors, that is, to be responsive to the subtle pressures from their political environment.

Another factor that links federal court judges to their political context is that they have often been involved in partisan politics prior to their appointment, and the partisan affiliations of judges is an important criterion in the selection process (Goldman 1975; Nagel 1961; Vines 1963; Carp and Rowland 1983).

My additional factor is that federal court judges may be responsive to political factors in their decision making in individual cases "due to the prospect of future promotion within the ranks of the judiciary or appointment to administrative positions" (Yarnold 1991b).

It is suggested that federal court judges decide cases with a view to future advancement within the judiciary or appointment to desirable positions outside of the judiciary. Hence, cases that come before judges are evaluated in terms of their political effects; for example, whether it is possible that a decision in a particular case will alienate a significant judicial constituency.

For example, in asylum-related appeals to the federal courts, federal court judges in high immigrant-flow areas were more inclined to rule in favor of litigants who claimed they were refugees than were judges in low immigrant-flow areas (Yarnold 1991b). Similarly, Baum (1989) suggests that courts are unlikely to adopt policies that fail to maintain minimum levels of social support. Cook (1981) found that sentencing decisions of federal court judges in draft cases were related to public opinion.

Another reason that federal court judges respond to political stimuli is that political actors become involved in federal court litigation. Many analysts have documented the fact that interest groups generally tend to have higher levels of success in litigation than non-organizational litigants (Galanter 1974, 1978; Dolbeare 1978; Epstein 1985; Wenner 1982; Wenner and Dutter 1988; Yarnold 1991b).

A somewhat surprising finding is that public interest groups were not involved as attorneys (either as representatives or as *amicus curiae*) for relators in federal court cases arising under 18 U.S.C. 3184–3190. Relators usually hired private attorneys to represent them in their extradition cases. This contrasts with other litigation areas, in which public interest groups become heavily involved on the behalf of individuals.

For example, in appeals to the federal courts (1980–87) from adverse decisions of agencies within the immigration bureaucracy on claims for political asylum and withholding of deportation, many aliens had public interest group involvement in their appeals, where the groups appeared either as representatives or as *amicus curiae* (Yarnold 1990a, 1991b). The involvement of these interest groups tended to increase the aliens' chances of prevailing in these cases. Similarly, in federal court decisions involving the environment, many public interest groups appeared to represent the public interest in an improved environment; these groups also tended to have high levels of success in litigation (Wenner 1982; Wenner and Dutter 1988).

In contrast, in not one of the 82 extradition cases examined in this analysis was there interest group involvement. The main problem for relators (or those subject to extradition) is that they are, in a very real sense, no one's constituents. Relators whose extradition was sought came from states worldwide. In the district court cases examined here there were fugitives from, among other states, Ireland, Italy, France, and Canada. Only rarely did a case involve a U.S. citizen whose extradition was sought by another state.

Since relators have few ties to the United States and may only reside here temporarily, they do not form a political constituency in the United States. In contrast to refugees, they are not likely to become permanent U.S. residents.

Hence, relators tend to be unorganized, and U.S. political representatives do not lobby on their behalf. There are no interest groups that lobby for their benefit or form for the purpose of providing them with *pro bono* (for free) legal representation.

The suggestion that relators are not a political constituency in the United States is borne out by the statistical analysis. Unlike asylum-related appeals, federal court outcomes in extradition cases are not related to the relative size of immigrant populations within judges' states. It was earlier argued that immigrants in the United States tend to identify with refugees. In contrast, the immigrant population probably does not identify to any great extent with those subject to extradition. Hence, there is no judicial constituency directly affected by the decisions of federal court judges in extradition cases that might, simply through its presence within judicial districts, pressure federal court judges to rule in favor of relators.

Because relators are ineligible to vote in the United States, political parties do not cater to their needs. Thus, it is not surprising that the partisanship variable is not related to outcome in extradition cases. Extradition is also not a major, conflictual issue that might generate partisan division. Democratic judges did not, for example, feel strongly inclined to rule in favor of relators. In fact, relators tended to lose more often in extradition cases in which the judges were linked to the Democratic Party.

Given the low saliency of international extradition as a political issue in the United States and the fact that it is a topic only rarely addressed by the news media, the general public is too uninformed (or apathetic) to have an opinion on extradition. Few, if any, interest groups lobby on the behalf of those subject to international extradition.

Members of issue networks (Heclo 1978) consisting primarily of legal scholars who specialize in the area of international law (for example, Bassiouni 1983; Higgins 1963; Rosenne 1973; Eagleton 1957) do express concern over the treatment of those subject to extradition, and even lobby in their favor (Bassiouni 1983), but these efforts tend to be sporadic and have little impact on policy making in the United States.

For example, during a hearing on the Extradition Act of 1981 (S. 1639) before the Senate Judiciary Committee, held on October 14, 1981, few interest groups offered testimony. This is particularly striking due to the nature of the changes in extradition practice that the executive branch had proposed, which included elimination of the judiciary's role in determining whether the political offense exception to extradition applies to specific relators. The amendments were in response to the fact that the federal courts had often, particularly in the case of Irish fugitives, upheld the political offense exception.

Only three interest groups were involved in these hearings and their comments tended to be brief; most opposed the proposed elimination of judicial authority over the political offense exception. Private attorneys also testified, and their support for the amendment was about evenly split. Two members of issue networks testified, both professors: M. Cherif Bassiouni, a member of the faculty of DePaul Law School (Chicago) and Christopher Pyle of Mount Holyoke College (South Hadley, Mass.). Both argued against eliminating the authority of the federal courts over the political offense exception and in favor of expanding the substantive and procedural rights of relators. (See the appendix to this chapter for a list of those who testified at the hearing.)

Those subject to extradition, or relators, do not form a political constituency in the United States and hence are not greatly assisted by interest groups, elected officials, or political parties.

The only exception to this rule occurs in the context of those extraditees who are members of an organization on whose behalf they committed a crime. Such relators tended to prevail more often in extradition cases arising in U.S. federal courts than did aliens with no such organizational link. While the average success level for relators in extradition cases was 26 percent, relators with links to external organizations prevailed in 40 percent of these cases (n = 5). However, the variable of linkage to an external organization is not statistically significant.

In previous analyses of federal court outcomes in asylum-related appeals (Yarnold 1990a, 1991b), it was argued that the involvement of organizations might lead to high levels of litigation success because organizations have superior litigation resources with which to argue the merits of a case (Galanter 1974, 1978), and because federal court judges respond to the political clout of these organizations.

In the extradition cases examined here there was no direct organizational involvement in the proceedings. Interest groups did not become involved on the behalf of relators either as legal representatives or as *amicus curiae*. Also, the external organizations on whose behalf relators committed crimes (for example, the PLO and the IRA) did not directly assist the relators in federal court proceedings.

As a result, the first advantage of organizational involvement, that organizations lend excellent litigation resources to individual litigants, is not relevant in this context. If organizational links still matter in extradition cases, it is not due to the superior litigation resources of organizations but to their political clout. Hence, we are left with a test of the extent to which federal court judges respond to the political clout of organizations to which individual litigants are linked.

Membership in an external organization, however, did not guarantee that relators would be more successful than litigants with no such organizational link. Relators who were linked to the PLO (or Abu Nidal) for example, fared worse on average than did relators with no external organizational memberships, prevailing in 0 percent of the cases (n = 2) although the overall success rate was 26 percent. In contrast, members of the IRA tended to prevail to a greater extent than did relators without organizational links, winning in 67 percent of the cases (n = 3).

How does one account for the higher success levels enjoyed by IRA members in extradition cases? Probably the best explanation lies in the fact that the IRA has an effective ethnic lobby group in the United States, while the PLO does not. Farrell (1985) traces the history of the Irish in the United States and the treatment of political refugees from Ireland who were members of the IRA by U.S. policy makers, including the courts.

The growth of a pro-IRA lobby in the United States was facilitated by the fact that there were huge flows of Irish immigrants to the United States. Farrell (1985) suggests that there was a huge influx of economic and political refugees from Ireland after the famine and the Young Ireland movement. Briggs (1984) estimates that between 1845 and 1855, 250,000 Irish immigrants migrated to the United States in the wake of a famine.

Byrne (1969) suggests that official estimates tended to underestimate Irish immigration to the United States. From 1820 (the date that official statistics on numbers and nationality of immigrants began to be kept) to 1872, four million Irish immigrants had come to the United States, while official estimates put the number at three million. The total number of immigrants to the United States during this period was approximately eight million. Byrne claims, "Until within a few years past, when the strong current of German immigration began to set in, the great majority of all immigrants were Irish" (Byrne 1969: 17).

Irish immigrants to the United States were also helped by a long-term bias of U.S. immigration policy in favor of immigrants from Western countries (Briggs 1984). This bias worked to the detriment of immigrants from, for example, Palestine. Palestinian immigrants to the United States comprised a minute fraction of all U.S. immigrants during the country's early history.

It is very difficult to measure Palestinian migration to the United States because the agency responsible for collecting immigration statistics, the Immigration and Naturalization Service, does not currently keep separate records of Palestinian migration to the United States. Instead, Palestinians who come to the United States are recorded as either Jordanian or Israeli immigrants. This may result from the fact that the state of Israel was formally founded in 1948, in what was Palestinian territory.

However, a publication of the U.S. Bureau of the Census (1975) lists the foreign-born population in the United States, by country of birth, from 1850 to 1970. Although after 1940 this source includes Palestinians in the category of "other Asia," these early statistics give some idea of the size of the Palestinian constituency in the United States. In 1920, the total foreign-born population in the United States was 13,920,692. The Irish-American community comprised approximately 7.4 percent (1,037,234) of this population, while there were only 3,203 Palestinians in the United States at this time, for a total of 0.02 percent of its foreign-born population.

By 1940, the foreign-born population in the United States had declined to 11,419,138. At this point, the Irish-American population numbered 678,447, for a total of 5.9 percent of the foreign-born population, while 7,047 Palestinians resided in the United States, representing 0.06 percent of the total (U.S. Bureau of the Census 1975).

In the 1950 census of the United States (U.S. Bureau of the Census 1954), a chart of "foreign-born white population by country of birth, by states, 1950," lists a total of 10,158,854 foreign-born whites in the United States. Of these, 540, or 0.005 percent, were from "Arab Palestine," as compared with 520,359 from Ireland, representing 5.1 percent of the total. Unfortunately, these reports also, after 1950, merge Palestinians into the category of "other Asia," so that it is difficult to measure more recent Palestinian migration to the United States.

It is possible to indirectly assess the current size of the Palestinian community in the U.S. by examining the number of Palestinian organizations that are listed in directories of U.S. organizations. One such directory, the *Encyclopedia of Associations 1990* (Burek, Koek, and Novallo 1990) lists Palestinian organizations in the United States. In a "Name and Keyword" index, under "Palestinian" and "Palestine," 55 different organizations were listed. This contrasts with 128 such organizations found under the words "Irish" and "Ireland."

Contact was made in May 1990 with a representative of one of the Palestinian organizations, the Palestine Affairs Center in Washington, D.C. A representative of the organization, Michel Jubran, indicated that the Palestinian community in the United States is small relative to other ethnic communities. He estimated that in 1990, the Palestinian community in the United States numbered about 1.2 million, although this estimate seems high in light of previous statistics on Palestinian migration to the United States.

He suggested that the Palestinian community in the United States had not been active in organizing, and that this is the "main weakness" of the Palestinian lobby. However, he noted that this community is becoming aware of the need to organize and is beginning to do do in a more effective manner.

Of course, Palestinians in the United States do get some indirect representation from the larger Arab community. However, the Arab community in the United States is also relatively small; one estimate placed it at 2.5 million in 1989 (Madison 1989). Although there is an Arab lobby in Washington, D.C., it has been characterized as a lobby that lacks constituents (Chomsky 1983; Madison 1989). It has also been criticized on the grounds that it is more anti-Israel in its lobbying than pro-Arab, and that it has immense difficulty attracting legislative supporters due to the (occasional) virulence of its lobbying and the fact that few congressmen are willing to alienate the strong Jewish lobby in the United States (Chomsky 1983; Madison 1989).

The Arab community tends to lobby in favor of major changes in U.S. policy toward Arab states. For example, it has mounted effective battles over the sale of military and surveillance equipment (the AWACs, for example) to individual Arab states. The Arab lobby may not be particularly concerned with the more immediate needs of the smaller Palestinian community in the United States, particularly when the issue becomes something as obscure as the extradition of Palestinians to other states (Madison 1989; Chomsky 1983).

In contrast, the fact that there was a supportive ethnic lobby in the United States worked to the advantage of many Irish dissidents who took refuge in the

United States. Farrell (1985) suggests that by as early as 1852, the Irish lobby in the U.S. was strong enough to frustrate attempts by British authorities to obtain the extradition of Irish fugitives in the U.S. For example, in 1852 Britain sought the extradition of an Irish national named Thomas Kaine (in New York) on a charge of attempted murder. It was alleged that Kaine shot at a man in Ireland who had taken over land from which another farmer had been evicted. According to Farrell (1985: 16):

> Kaine was not brought to court "for fear that he would be rescued from the custody of the law by a mob." In 1853 a circuit court judge ordered his release mainly on the grounds that there was insufficient evidence to establish a *prima facie* case against him.

A more significant Irish case arose 50 years later, in 1903, when an Irish fugitive, James Lynchehaun, was arrested on a warrant seeking his extradition. Some years earlier Lynchehaun had been convicted in Ireland for the attempted murder of his former landlord. He escaped from prison and fled to the United States (Farrell 1985).

The Irish community in the United States mobilized around the Lynchehaun case since members viewed it as vital to all Irish political refugees: "Lynchehaun was the first convicted prisoner for whom an extradition warrant had been issued" (Farrell 1985: 20). According to Farrell, the Irish community believed the case might set an important precedent for future refugees from Ireland. Hence, a defense committee was formed within the Irish-American community with the objective of establishing a "sacred right: the right of asylum for political offenders" (Farrell 1985).

In his defense, Lynchehaun claimed that the attempted murder of his landlord, Mrs. MacDonnell, was politically motivated. He testified that he was a member of the Land League in Ireland (an organization of tenants who were opposed to landlords) and that the organization planned to kill Mrs. MacDonnell due to her harsh treatment of tenants. Other Irish witnesses reinforced his testimony. Defense lawyers argued that the crime was part of a broad movement that sought to overthrow the established political and social order and that it was intimately linked to the Irish struggle for self-government (Farrell 1985).

British authorities countered that the offense was purely personal and that Lynchehaun had previously worked as an agent for Mrs. MacDonnell. Farrell (1985) indicates that Lynchehaun had a violent reputation, and suggests that his motivation was probably mainly personal. Nevertheless, "his witnesses convinced the court that there had been sort of a popular uprising against Mrs. MacDonnell on the night in question" (Farrell 1985: 20).

The U.S. commissioner who was presiding over the case, Charles W. Moore, agreed with defense attorneys and ordered the release of Lynchehaun. The commissioner held:

The real test lies deeper than definitions. It is this: Would the crime have been done had there been no political motive? Would the fire and the ensuing riot have occurred save for the long chain of moving causes that preceded it—the discontent of the tenants as a class, the agrarian agitation. (Farrell 1985: 21–22)

Although arguably weak on the merits, the Lynchehaun case set important precedents: the United States would become a place of refuge for political refugees from Ireland and U.S. courts would not comply with extradition requests when the political offense exception was raised as a defense.

Farrell suggests that "the United States had been the traditional refuge of Irish political fugitives from the 1798 Rebellion to the aftermath of the Civil War" (Farrell 1985: 80). However, the nature of Irish fugitives changed, from members of the Land League, who primarily sought to displace landlords, to immigrants who were more dangerous to British interests. For example, after 1945, members of the IRA who had been active in Ireland during the 1940s and 1950s came to the United States. Leaders of the IRA went to the United States as well, including Sean Cronin (chief of staff of the IRA), and Liam Kelly (head of Saor Uladh) (Farrell 1985).

Farrell explains that at this point, the British government made no attempt to extradite these individuals, even though their location and activities in the United States were well known:

The United States courts had strengthened the tradition of the political exception since the Ezeta and Lynchehaun cases at the turn of the century. In the Cold War hysteria of the 1950s they had even extended it to cover acts that most people would regard as war crimes and genocide in a case where the perpetrator was sought by a Communist government. (Farrell 1985: 80)

The nationalist revolt in Northern Ireland, which began in 1969, triggered a new wave of sympathy from Irish-Americans. The Irish-American community mobilized to give shelter to IRA members who came to the United States and also became a critical source of weapons and funds for the IRA.

British authorities responded to this new crisis by increased lobbying of the U.S. government. The U.S. administration attempted to placate its ally by taking steps against gun-running and refusing to grant visas to IRA members.

Nevertheless, the U.S. courts continued to recognize the political offense exception in several important cases involving Irish fugitives in the 1970s and 1980s (Farrell 1985). One such case involved William Joseph Quinn (*Quinn v. Robinson*, No. C-82-6688 PPA; N. D. Cal. Oct. 3, 1983), whose extradition was sought by the British government. British authorities charged Quinn with murdering a policeman in London, conspiring to cause explosions, and sending letter bombs to British public officials.

Quinn was a U.S. citizen, although his parents were both Irish-Americans. He left the United States in 1971 and went to Ireland to join the IRA. The organization sent him to London to carry out a number of bombings. He was, however, arrested by British authorities in 1975. After serving a one-year prison sentence in Ireland for his membership in the IRA, Quinn returned to the United States. In 1981, British authorities sought his extradition from the United States, but Quinn countered that his criminal activities in London, including the murder of a policeman, were political offenses that were carried out as a part of a larger campaign by the IRA (Farrell 1985).

In 1982, a magistrate rejected Quinn's plea. However, the case was reviewed by Judge Robert P. Aguilar in a federal district court in California. In October 1983, he ruled in favor of Quinn and denied extradition. He held that the bombings carried out by Quinn were incidental to, and occurred in the course of, a political uprising of the IRA against the British and hence fell within the political offense exception to extradition (Farrell 1985).

Judge Aguilar gave a powerful rebuff to U.S. government attorneys who had argued during the case that decisions relating to the political offense exception are properly made by the executive. Judge Aguilar suggested that leaving decisions on the political offense exception to the judiciary ensured that such decisions would not be influenced by

> political considerations such as the favour due or not due to the country seeking extradition, or the sympathy to the political position of the person whose extradition is sought. Until Congress decides that such political considerations should be part of the determination . . . the judiciary must guardedly preserve its role in making unbiased and independent decisions on the applicability of the . . . exception. (Farrell 1985: 88–89)

The decision in Quinn's case contrasts sharply with the treatment afforded a member of the PLO, in the case of *Abu Eain v. Wilkes*, 641 F.2d 504 (7th Cir. 1981), where the court held that the political offense exception did not apply. Abu Eain was a Palestinian who lived in the Israeli-occupied West Bank area. He was arrested in Chicago in 1979. Israel sought his extradition, claiming that he was responsible for planting a bomb at a youth rally in 1979; the explosion killed two schoolboys and wounded thirty-six others. He claimed that the bombing was part of a plan of activity organized by the PLO (Farrell 1985).

According to Farrell, in rejecting the Palestinian's political offense plea, the court narrowed the very broad interpretation of the political offense exception that was earlier adopted in *Karadzole v. Artukovic* and had been applied in the Quinn case. However, the court in this case found there was no clear connection between overthrowing the Israeli government and the random bombing of civilians by Abu Eain. It ruled:

> The exception does not make a random bombing intended to result in the cold-blooded murder of civilians incidental to a purpose of toppling

a government, absent a direct link between the perpetrator, a political organization's political goals, and the specific act. (Farrell 1985)

The Artukovic case, in contrast, suggests that to qualify as a political offense, "the crime must be incidental to and form a part of political disturbances. It must be in furtherance of one side or another of a bona fide struggle for political power" (Farrell 1985: 81).

The difference in litigation success between members of the IRA who are fugitives—who tend to be very successful—and Palestinian fugitives affiliated with the PLO, who tend not to prevail in extradition cases, may be attributed to the fact that IRA members have a sympathetic, organized and powerful lobby of Irish Americans in the United States while members of the PLO do not.

Also at a disadvantage in extradition cases are relators with no links to external organizations. Many of these tend to be common criminals having, for example, embezzled funds from their countries of origin. Extradition requests in these cases were overwhelmingly granted. In the 86 extradition cases examined in this analysis, almost three-quarters (64, or 74 percent) of all cases represented losses for relators.

Conclusion

Ethnic politics in the United States seems to have had an effect on the decision making of the presumably apolitical federal courts in extradition cases. Irish fugitives who were members of the IRA and have the support of a powerful ethnic lobby in the United States tended to prevail in extradition cases to a greater extent that did others who did not have the benefit of a supportive ethnic lobby. Members of the PLO tended to be far less successful in extradition cases than were their Irish counterparts. Hence, ethnic politics carried over into the policy-making arena of the lower federal courts.

To the extent that extradition decisions of the U.S. federal district courts are based on political factors, there is evidence that individuals subject to extradition proceedings in national court systems are not receiving fair trials and that their nationally and internationally recognized substantive and procedural rights are being impaired.

There is no reason to expect that the courts of the United States are exceptional in this regard, which suggests that national courts ought not have any role in the adjudication of extradition cases. Public interest groups might form within countries for the purpose of lobbying on the behalf of those subject to extradition proceedings.

Appendix

Hearing before the Committee on the Judiciary of the United States Senate, 97th Congress, 1st Session, October 14, 1981, on the Extradition Act of 1981, or S. 1639.

Individuals and Organizations Who Gave Statements at Hearing on S. 1639

1. American Civil Liberties Union
2. Romeo T. Capulong, chairman of the Human Rights Committee of the Philippine-American Lawyers Association of New York
3. Dante C. Simbulan, executive director, Ad Hoc Coalition on Extradition
4. Professor M.Cherif Bassiouni, School of Law, DePaul University
5. Professor Christopher Pyle, Mount Holyoke College
6. William M. Hanney, attorney at law (Chicago)
7. William M. Goodman, attorney at law (San Francisco)
8. Abdeen M. Jabara, attorney at law (Detroit)
9. James R. Streiker, attorney at law (Chicago)
10. Thomas P. Sullivan, attorney at law (Chicago)
11. Michael A. Abbell, Director, Office of International Affairs, Criminal Division, Department of Justice

3

Contextual Variables: Region

CASE STUDY 4: REGION VERSUS POLITICS IN FEDERAL COURT ABORTION CASES

Roe's Progeny: Federal District Court Outcomes in Abortion Cases, 1973–90

Previous research (Yarnold 1990a, 1990b, 1991a) found that region was not a significant factor in court cases dealing with refugees, asylees, and international extradition. In an attempt to reconcile this conclusion with previous findings that region was related to outcome, for example, in environmental cases (Wenner 1982; Wenner and Dutter 1988), and race relations cases (Richardson and Vines 1978), I suggested that regional effects might be most apparent in cases that deal with a highly ideological issue, such as abortion.

This analysis examines the extent to which federal district court judges, in their decisions in abortion cases from 1973 to 1990, have served to enhance the abortion rights of women, first given protection by the Supreme Court in *Roe v. Wade*, 410 U.S. 113 (1973). It also examines the extent to which these decisions are related to political, factual, and regional variables.

Hypotheses

Although the judiciary is often viewed as a passive interpreter of the law, federal court judges examined in this analysis were not unduly restrained in their decision making by the law, due to the vagueness of standards they were called on to interpret. In abortion cases from 1973 to 1990 that rely on *Roe v. Wade*

(1973) as a precedent, federal district courts were required to apply the holding of *Roe* to state and federal laws being challenged and determine whether they had unconstitutionally infringed abortion rights. However, as is often the case in judicial decision making, there is great ambiguity in the language of *Roe*. Hence, there are few standards that bind judges to employ uniform criteria in their decision making.

To comprehend the *Roe* decision and the controversy it engendered, it is necessary to examine first the precedent on which *Roe* relied, which set forth the privacy right. This precedent is the Supreme Court's decision in *Griswold v. Connecticut*, 381 U.S. 479 (1965). Griswold, the executive director of the Planned Parenthood League of Connecticut, was convicted under a state statute that made the use of contraceptives a criminal offense and also punished accessories who, like Griswold, provided information, instruction, and advice to married couples to prevent pregnancies through contraception. Joined as a codefendant was a professor of the Yale Medical School, who served as medical director of the Planned Parenthood League of Connecticut. According to one account (Garraty 1987), Planned Parenthood had been attempting to change the state law banning contraceptives for decades but had been successfully opposed by a powerful bloc of Catholic state legislators that halted all efforts at reform.

An initial observation is that powerful interest groups in the United States were affected by the Supreme Court's decisions in *Griswold* (*Roe*'s precursor) and in *Roe* as well. These groups played a role in shaping the Supreme Court's agenda and rulings in both cases and undoubtedly benefited from their litigation exposure and experience in this issue, which derived from decades of involvement in privacy- and abortion-related litigation.

The defendants in the *Griswold* case admitted violating the state law in question. To avoid prosecution, the defendants claimed the state law violated their privacy rights protected by the due process clause of the Fourteenth Amendment. However, as Justices Black and Stewart suggested in their dissent, there is no explicit privacy right set forth in the Constitution. The defendants countered by arguing that the privacy right was an implicit right that emanated from "penumbras" found in certain provisions of the Bill of Rights. In one of the most problematic cases ever faced by law students in their relentless search for "black letter law," the Supreme Court, in an opinion delivered by Justice Douglas, recognized the right to privacy and held that it was violated by the state statute that banned the use of contraceptives. A portion of that opinion is as follows:

> The foregoing cases suggest that specific guarantees in the Bill of Rights have penumbras, formed by emanations from those guarantees that help give them life and substance. . . .
>
> Various guarantees create zones of privacy. The right of association contained in the penumbra of the First Amendment is one. . . . The Third Amendment in its prohibition against the quartering of soldiers "in any

house" in time of peace without the consent of the owner is another facet of that privacy. (*Griswold v. Connecticut*, 381 U.S. 479, 1973)

In this paragraph, the court cited the First, Third, Fourth, Fifth, and Ninth amendments in its search for the extra-constitutional privacy right and, in the process, created a new constitutional lingo that sent legal scholars in search of "penumbras." Nevertheless, for the purpose of *Roe* and pro-abortion litigation groups, *Griswold* set forth the important precedent that a constitutional right of privacy exists.

By the time *Roe* reached the Supreme Court in 1973, a strong pro-abortion coalition had formed in the United States consisting of groups of medical professionals who had been, in some cases, performing abortions in violation of the law and who sought to legalize the practice. Also involved were women's rights organizations, civil liberties groups, and population control groups, among others (Garraty 1987). The opposition, consisting primarily of conservative religious groups, was not well organized at this point.

In 1973, the Supreme Court in *Roe v. Wade*, 410 U.S. 113, and the companion case of *Doe v. Bolton*, 410 U.S. 179, relied on the privacy right set forth earlier in *Griswold* to hold that the Fourteenth Amendment due process clause and the "privacy right" had been violated by Texas and Georgia laws that banned abortions except where necessary to save the mother's life (Texas law) or where the pregnancy would endanger the life of the mother or seriously injure her health (Georgia law). The immediate result of this ruling was that the abortion laws of 46 states and Washington, D.C., were invalidated (Wolpert and Rosenberg 1990).

Justice Blackmun drafted and delivered the opinion in *Roe v. Wade* (1973), which was supported by seven members of the Supreme Court. Blackmun recognized that the state of Texas had a legitimate interest in regulating abortions to protect both maternal and fetal life. However, state interests had to be weighed against the privacy interests of women, which accorded them the right to termination of an early pregnancy. In Blackmun's words: "We therefore conclude that the right of privacy includes the abortion decision, but that this right is not unqualified and must be considered against important state interests in regulation" (*Roe v. Wade* 1973).

The decision was ultimately based on the Supreme Court's resolution of the issue of when a state's interest in protecting maternal and fetal life becomes sufficiently compelling to warrant state regulation of abortion. The state law, it will be recalled, banned all abortions unless necessary to save the life of the mother. In response to the issue of the state interest in maternal life, the decision provides:

With respect to the State's important and legitimate interest in the health of the mother, the "compelling" point, in light of the present medical knowledge, is at approximately the end of the first trimester. This is so because of the now established medical fact . . . that until the end of the first trimester mortality in abortion is less than mortality in normal childbirth. It follows that, from and after this point, a State may regulate the abortion procedure to the extent that the regulation reasonably relates to the preservation and protection of human health. (*Roe v. Wade* 1973)

Hence, future judges, when considering the legitimacy of a law that regulates post-first trimester abortions enacted to foster maternal health, are called on to determine if the regulation "reasonably relates" to its stated goal; this is certainly a vague standard.

Even more problematic is the determination as to when a state's interest in protecting fetal life becomes compelling. The opinion reads: "With respect to the State's important and legitimate interest in potential life, the 'compelling' point is at viability. This is so because the fetus then presumably has the capability of meaningful life outside the mother's womb" (*Roe v. Wade* 1973).

On the basis of medical testimony, Blackmun had earlier concluded that "viability is usually placed at about seven months (28 weeks) but may occur earlier, even at 24 weeks."

Prior to viability, or during the first trimester of pregnancy, states are severely limited in their ability to regulate abortions: "If the State is interested in protecting fetal life after viability, it may go so far as to proscribe abortion during that period except when it is necessary to preserve the life or health of the mother" (*Roe v. Wade*, 1973).

Hence, courts are given the rather vague message that first trimester regulation is highly suspect, yet after this point regulation may be acceptable if "necessary to preserve the life or health of the mother." Distinguishing between laws that meet this first trimester standard and those that do not is indeed a formidable task.

In making the determination as to when a fetus becomes viable, and whether maternal life is more endangered by childbirth than abortion, the Supreme Court was entirely dependent on expert testimony. Testimony on both issues, but particularly on the question of fetal viability, was substantial and conflicting (Garraty 1987).

Some suggest that the Supreme Court should not attempt to make determinations, such as whether an infant is viable, that greatly rely on scientific and medical expertise (Blank 1984). As Blank suggests:

It is argued here that the courts are put in a difficult position when they base decisions on biological rationale, especially when they fail to recognize or understand the extent to which technological advances are altering biological "fact." These controversies have an "inherently hybrid technical and legal character" and "present issues that can be resolved by neither purely technical nor purely legal analysis." . . . These issues force the courts to deal not only with new forms of information but also with new methods of analysis for understanding causality which are totally alien to the language and mode of analysis of the legal profession. It is not surprising, therefore, that these new demands on the courts produce severe strain as well. (Blank 1984: 584–85)

It should come as no surprise, given the vagueness of the underlying standards for abortion cases, that judicial decisions have been attacked as arbitrary and, in some cases, biased. Many critics contend that abortion is a highly politicized issue (Hildreth and Dran 1990). As a result, they suggest, judicial decisions relating to abortion are not immune to political pressure. For example, Sackett (1985) asserts that the Supreme Court issued a decision in *Roe v. Wade* that paralleled public preferences.

As a result of their discretion, courts substitute their own standards for vague legal and constitutional standards. Hence, federal court outcomes may be related to variables that have little to do with the law or the facts of a case. The following discussion reviews several extraneous independent variables drawn from public law research that have been found in previous analyses to be related to judicial outcomes.

Political Variables

Political variables may be significantly related to district court outcomes in abortion cases. This suggestion may seem anomalous, given that federal courts are generally viewed as immune to political influences because their members have been appointed for life and socialized into objectivity.

However, in the same way that courts have been shown to engage in policy making and not merely legal interpretation, many analysts concede that judicial decision making is often linked to political factors. Judges do not operate in a vacuum and may be influenced by their environment, including their political environment. Hence, judicial outcomes have been linked to such political factors as the involvement of groups in litigation, the partisan affiliation of judges, public opinion, and constituency preferences.

From previous analysis, it is expected that federal court outcomes will be linked to political factors in two types of cases: (1) where the issue is major, publicized, and on which constituents have preferences that serve to restrict policy makers (Case Studies 1 and 2, Chapter 2; Yarnold 1990a, 1990b); and (2) where the litigation issue is not a major one, yet it affects the interests of politically powerful groups within the United States (Case Study 3, Chapter 2; Yarnold 1991a).

Political Party. If judges are influenced by political variables, perhaps district court outcomes in abortion cases are related to the partisan affiliation of the judges involved or the partisan affiliation of their appointing presidents (Baum 1989); Goldman 1975; Nagel 1961; Vines 1963; Yarnold 1990a, 1990b, 1991; Carp and Rowland 1983). The Republican Party, since the Supreme Court's ruling in *Roe v. Wade*, has identified itself with an anti-abortion stance, whereas Democrats were quick to adopt a pro-abortion position (Appleton 1981; Horan 1981; Segers 1982; Granberg 1985; Bolce 1988). Although some Republican politicians drifted into the pro-abortion camp towards the end of the 1980s, abortion may still be an issue that leads to partisan division. Hence, it is expected that Democratic judges will more likely enter a pro-abortion ruling than will Republican judges.

Interest Group Litigation. Interest groups lobby the courts through their direct involvement in litigation (Yarnold 1990a, 1990b). Hence, another political variable that many assert affects federal court outcomes is the involvement of organized interests in litigation. In the federal district court abortion cases included in this analysis, two categories of interest groups became involved, either as *amicus curiae* or as representatives: pro-abortion and anti-abortion interest groups. The analysis examines the extent to which the involvement of pro- and anti-abortion interest groups in litigation affects the outcome in abortion cases.

Judicial Constituencies and Public Opinion. Another political variable that may affect state court judges is public opinion (Cook 1981; Baum 1989), or the preferences of judicial constituents (Yarnold 1990a, 1990b, 1991a).

In evaluating the link between policy making and constituency preferences, one must address the question of which constituency of the decision maker might be most directly affected by the decision in question (Yarnold 1990a, 1990b, 1991a). In abortion cases, the constituency most likely to be affected by judicial decisions is women. As Scott and Schuman (1988) suggest, pro-abortion women regard the abortion issue as more important than do pro-abortion men because it is women, both individually and collectively, who stand to lose most by abortion restrictions. Similarly, for those who oppose abortion, the Supreme Court's legal sanction of this practice is viewed as a threat to traditional morality and the family unit (Petchesky 1984; Luker 1984; Clarke 1987; Scott and Schuman 1988). Hildreth and Dran (1990) suggest that abortion might be an issue on which women coalesce, and hence, women may be a significant judicial constituency in abortion decisions. The presence of a politically powerful female constituency in judges' states may influence judicial outcomes.

One way to assess the political clout of women in states is to measure the percentage of federal congressional seats (for both the Senate and the House) that are held by women in the year in which a decision is rendered. I expect that district court judges from states with a high percentage of female congressional representatives will more likely adopt a pro-abortion position in abortion cases than will judges in states with a low percentage of female congressmen. This variable was obtained by combining data on women in Congress provided by the Center for the American Woman and Politics (CAWP, National Information Data Bank on Women in Public Office, Eagleton Institute of Politics, Rutgers University) and *Congressional Quarterly* (1988, 1973–90).

Competing Hypotheses

Although conceding that courts are policy makers, unconstrained by the law and facts of a case, other analysis suggest that court outcomes are linked to environmental variables, and that these variables explain the variance in judicial outcomes as much as or more than do political variables.

Region. Geographic region has often been cited as a contextual variable that affects judicial decision making. Carp and Rowland (1983) showed that judicial decisions in the South and West were more conservative than those rendered in the North and Midwest. Richardson and Vines (1978) point out that judges in the South were the least sympathetic to civil rights litigants. Cook (1978) discovered that the most severe sentencing decisions were rendered by federal district judges in the South. Wenner (1982) also found that in environmental litigation, region was related to judicial decision making. Later, Wenner and Dutter (1988) suggest that region continued to affect these outcomes, and that in district court cases involving environmental litigation, pro-environment groups enjoyed the most support from judges in the Northeast (circuits 1, 2, and 3), followed by judges in the Midwest (circuits 6, 7, and 8). Lower levels of support were exhibited by judges in the South (circuits 4, 5, and 11); judges in the West (circuits 9 and 10) were divided in their support of pro-environment groups.

Hence, a first competing hypothesis is that geographic region is significantly linked to judicial outcomes in the abortion cases involved in this analysis.

Fact Variable: State versus Federal Law

It has also been suggested that judicial outcomes are related to the important facts of a case (Segal 1985; Gibson 1977; Dudley 1989; Gryski et al. 1986; Haire and Songer 1990). One fact that may be important in abortion cases is whether the abortion law being challenged is a federal or state policy. Some analysts suggest that the activism of the federal judiciary is more apparent when state laws are being challenged, as opposed to federal laws, as evidenced by the fact that state laws are overturned by the federal judiciary at a much higher rate than are federal laws (Baum 1989). Hence, this variable is included as a second control variable.

Data and Methods

Data for this analysis consist of the progeny of *Roe v. Wade*, 410 U.S. 113 (1973), or federal district court cases that cite *Roe* in their decisions. The district court cases included were decided after January 22, 1973, the date of the Supreme Court's decision in *Roe*, to the end of 1990. These 145 cases were found in the *Federal Supplement*, an official source for federal district court cases. An additional case was excluded from the analysis because it was decided by the D.C. district court, and hence could not be properly coded on the region variable.

The dependent variable is whether the decision is pro-abortion, broadly construed as a decision that promotes the abortion rights of women as set forth in *Roe v. Wade* (1973). This is a dichotomous variable, which suggests that standard regression analysis, with its assumption that the dependent variable is continuous, is not appropriate for our purposes. Although most of the cases were presided over by one judge, in some cases, the panel included up to three judges.

The first independent variable, the partisan affiliation of judges or, more precisely, the partisan affiliation of their appointing presidents, is measured by the percentage of judges involved in a district court case who were appointed by a Democratic president. This variable has been dichotomized at its mean: 47 percent of all judges involved in the 145 district court cases were appointed by a Democratic president. One complication is that, as mentioned, some of these cases were decided by only one judge while others were decided by a panel of up to three judges. For the purposes of measurement, when one district court judge is presiding and was appointed by a Democratic president, this case is coded on the partisanship variable as 100 percent of judges appointed by a Democratic president. If three judges are presiding, and one of the judges was appointed by a Democratic president, this case is coded as 33 percent of judges appointed by a Democratic president.

The involvement of interest groups in the federal district court abortion cases is measured by examining the written decisions for each of these cases, which typically list whether interest groups are involved. The groups involved are then coded in terms of whether they are pro- or anti-abortion. Interest groups are included whether they appear in a representative capacity or as *amicus curiae*.

To assess the strength of women as a judicial constituency, a measure was taken of the percentage of congresswomen (including both senators and representatives) in the state in which the district court is located covering the years 1973–90, during which the decision was rendered. The data on congresswomen were obtained from the Center for the American Woman and Politics (Eagleton Institute of Politics). The data on the congressional delegations of individual states were found in reports on Congress (*Congressional Quarterly* 1988; 1973–89).

Statistical analysis consists of probit analysis, since the dependent variable—whether the decision is pro-abortion—is continuous and there are multiple independent variables. Probit analysis allows one to examine the relationship between multiple independent variables and a dependent variable when controlling for the other variables. Probit analysis has been successfully employed in previous analysis of court decision making (Yarnold 1990a, 1990b, 1991a; Wenner and Dutter 1988; Segal 1984).

Findings: Relationships between District Court Abortion Decisions and the Independent Variables

After deleting the insignificant regional variable of "South," the results of probit analysis are contained in Table 3.1.

The only statistically significant independent variables are the involvement of pro-abortion groups in litigation (p = 0.005) and the location of a district court in the West (p = 0.05), one political variable and one regional variable. The overall equation lacks statistical significance (p = 0.56).

With regard to the insignificant variables, most of the results conform with earlier speculation about the relationship between the independent variables and

Table 3.1
Probit Estimates for District Court Abortion Cases, 1973–90

Dependent Variable: Was Decision Pro-Choice?

Mean: 77%

Variable	Maximum Likelihood Estimate (MLE)	Standard Error (SE)	MLE/SE	
Constant	5.24	0.65	8.03	
High % Democratic Judges	0.05	0.25	0.20	
Pro-Choice Groups	0.77	0.25	3.02	**
Pro-Life Groups	-0.07	0.42	-0.16	
High % Women In Congress	-0.30	0.26	-1.16	
Court In North	-0.39	0.43	-0.91	
Court In Midwest	-0.62	0.40	-1.54	
Court In West	-1.00	0.53	-1.90	*
State Crime	0.71	0.49	1.45	

Chi-Square = 32.08   DF = 34   P = 0.56
N = 145

**Significant at 0.005
*Significant at 0.05

district court outcomes in abortion cases. Hence, Democratic judges (or judges appointed by Democratic presidents) were more likely to take a pro-abortion position in their rulings, the involvement of anti-abortion groups in litigation tended to decrease the likelihood of a pro-abortion decision, and the fact that a case involved state rather than federal law increased the probability that the law would be found unconstitutional.

However, there were surprises. The presence of a high percentage of congresswomen in a judge's state decreased (rather than increased) the probability that judges in that state would take a pro-abortion position. These findings thus suggest that judges did not take into account the possibly pro-abortion positions of politically powerful women in their states. Alternately, the measure of this judicial constituency variable may be flawed, or the position of women on the abortion issue may be divided between pro- and anti-abortion camps, thus giving no clear direction to policy makers, including judges.

Other surprises were that pro-abortion litigants were damaged when their cases were presided over by district courts in the North (insignificant), Midwest (insignificant), and West (significant). Previous probit analysis that included the South suggests that only this regional variable has a positive relationship with the dependent variable. Pro-abortion litigants were more likely to win in the South and were likely to face the greatest opposition from, in descending order, judges from the West, Midwest, and North.

The analysis reveals that pro-abortion judicial decisions are linked to the involvement of pro-abortion groups and the location of district courts in the West. Judicial outcomes, however, were not significantly related to other political variables: the partisanship of judges (or that of their appointing presidents); the involvement of anti-abortion groups in litigation; and the presence of a politically powerful group of congresswomen in judges' states (as a measure of a judicial constituency in abortion cases).

Other facts about these cases warrant inspection. Most notable is the huge involvement of interest groups, both pro- and anti-abortion, in these cases: 66 percent of the cases (96 of 145) had interest group involvement. However, the anti-abortion forces were overwhelmed by the much higher involvement of pro-abortion groups. Pro-abortion groups were involved in 65 percent (or 94 of 145 cases) of the cases, as compared with only 10 percent (or 14 out of 145 cases) for anti-abortion groups. Hence, pro-abortion groups enjoyed a 6.5 to 1 advantage over anti-abortion forces, a fact that was linked to highly favorable court outcomes for the pro-abortion forces. A pro-abortion decision was entered in 77 percent (111 of 145) of the abortion cases.

Pro-abortion groups appear to have a very well-organized (and well-funded) litigation strategy, and they benefit from cooperative litigation efforts between pro-abortion women's groups, groups of health-care providers who often have a financial interest in liberal abortion laws (such as abortion clinics), and civil rights groups. For example, a pro-abortion position was often advocated by local affiliates of the American Civil Liberties Union (ACLU) and the Center for Constitutional Rights, both broad-based civil liberties organizations that serve as watchdogs of the civil rights of all groups in the United States, not only women. Other groups specifically dedicated to the protection of women's rights were also quite active in these cases, such as the National Organization for Women (NOW). Associations of health-care providers also were involved, aware of the enormous risks to women from illegal abortions and of their own increasing financial stake in the provision of abortions. Many local abortion clinics and groups of health-care providers became advocates of women in these cases, as did more powerful national organizations such as Planned Parenthood, the National Medical Association, the National Association of Social Workers, and the American Public Health Association, among others. Other groups were also involved, though not with as great frequency, in making pro-abortion arguments, such as various religious organizations (the Religious Coalition for Abortion Rights) and pro-bono legal services providers (New Hampshire Legal Assistance).

Previous research (Yarnold 1990b) shows that success in litigation is significantly linked to cooperative litigation efforts by interest groups. Undoubtedly, pro-abortion forces enjoyed this advantage in federal court abortion cases examined in this analysis. This advantage was not, however, shared by anti-abortion groups. While it was not at all unusual to have more than one group involved in an abortion case on the pro-abortion side, the involvement by anti-abortion groups tended to be solo appearances, with a small number of groups representing the anti-abortion side. The same groups tended to surface in these cases: the Constitutional Right to Life Committee, Operation Rescue, Advocates for Life, Celebrate Life, Americans United for Life Legal Defense Fund, and various ad hoc or local groups such as Minnesota Citizens for Life, Care Center of Springfield, the Georgia Right to Life Committee, and Christians in Action. Most often, however, anti-abortion groups did not appear in these cases.

Region is another statistically significant variable. Courts in the West tended to rule against litigants advocating a pro-abortion position ($p = 0.05$). However, only 8 percent ($n = 12$) of the abortion cases were decided in the West. The South was also underrepresented in these cases: only 16 percent ($n = 23$) of the abortion cases were adjudicated by courts in the South. Over two-thirds of the cases were decided in the Midwest (47 percent, $n = 68$), and the North (29 percent, $n = 42$), where pro-abortion arguments were not always successful. However, given that 94 percent of the cases (or 136 of 145) involve a challenge to state law, and that the pro-abortion position prevailed in 77 percent of all cases, the typical case was one decided in a district court in the Midwest or North, which involved pro-abortion interest groups that mounted a successful challenge to a state abortion law. Hence, it appears that federal district court judges throughout the United States were very active in these abortion cases in whipping policy makers and judges in the Midwest and North into conformity with the national norm for abortion rights set forth by the U.S. Supreme Court in *Roe v. Wade* (1973).

Discussion

Statistical analysis reveals that two variables are significantly related to outcome in federal district court abortion cases decided from January 22, 1973, to 1990. One of these variables is political: the involvement of pro-abortion interest groups in litigation. The involvement of these interest groups increased the probability that judges would enter a pro-abortion decision in the abortion cases examined in this analysis. Federal court outcomes in these cases were also significantly linked to one regional variable: the location of the federal court in the West.

From previous analysis, it was expected that federal court outcomes would be linked to political factors in two types of cases: (1) where the issue is major, publicized, and on which constituents have preferences that serve to restrict policy makers (Case Studies 1 and 2, Chapter 2; Yarnold 1990a, 1990b); and (2) where the litigation issue is not a major one, yet it affects the interests of politically powerful groups within the United States (Case Study 3, Chapter 2; Yarnold 1991).

Both of these conditions are met in the context of abortion cases. First, abortion is a "major" issue, if one defines a "major" issue as one that is "institutionalized in party cleavages and linked to broad ideology among the public, where opinions are fairly firmly held and information about congressmen [judges] is easily obtainable" (Page et al. 1984: 753).

The abortion issue did lead to deep partisan division in the United States. In 1976, the two major parties adopted opposing positions on abortion, with Democrats on the pro-abortion side and Republicans supporting an anti-abortion position (Bolce 1988; Granberg 1985). By 1980, the difference sharpened between the Republican and Democratic platforms on the abortion issue (Bolce 1988). Ronald Reagan, the 1980 presidential nominee of the Republican Party, was regarded as staunchly anti-abortion and was supported by anti-abortion groups such as the National Right to Life Committee. President Jimmy Carter, the Democratic nominee, was committed to a pro-abortion position (Granberg 1985). George Bush, the Republican candidate for president, called in April 1989 for a constitutional amendment banning abortion; Michael Dukakis, the Democratic nominee, was strongly pro-abortion (*The Economist* 1989).

From the above, it appears that the abortion issue is "institutionalized in party cleavages" (Page et al. 1984) and from this perspective qualifies as a major issue. It also is an issue "linked to broad ideology among the public, where opinions are fairly firmly held" (Page et al. 1984), and information about decisions of policy makers is readily available. Graber (1990) suggests that the abortion issue is linked to broad public conceptions about the proper role of women in society: homemaker versus career woman. The availability of abortions, according to some, promotes promiscuity and hence endangers the traditional homemaker role of women. Others (Johnson et al. 1990) agree, noting that the abortion movement in the United States is divided on cultural grounds, with traditionalists bitterly opposed by libertarians.

By 1980, abortion had been legal for over seven years, yet it remained controversial (Granberg 1985). According to some commentators, legalized abortion was the most explosive and polarizing issue of the 1980s (Bolce 1988; Blank 1984). Blank goes even further, suggesting that abortion continues to be the kind of issue that "once or twice in a century . . . arises so divisive in nature, so far-reaching in its consequences, and so deep in its foundation that it calls every person to take a stand" (Blank 1984: 585).

Even if abortion were not a major issue, one might expect federal court outcomes in abortion cases to be politicized due to the existence of numerous interest groups, both pro- and anti-abortion, that are affected by decisions in these cases. In fact, the collective action of interest groups around the abortion issue led to the development of first, in the 1980s, a vigorous anti-abortion movement, followed by, toward the end of the 1980s, the resurgence of a powerful pro-abortion movement.

Sackett (1985) describes the Supreme Court's ruling in *Roe v. Wade*, 410 U.S. 113 (1973) and the court's ruling in the companion case of *Doe v. Bolton*, 410 U.S. 179 (1973) as a great shock to anti-abortion forces in the United States, which was not an organized group in 1973. She adds that these twin rulings, which had the effect of sanctioning abortion on demand, moved many interest groups in the United States to band together to protest what seemed to be the court's outrageous and immoral act.

From 1973 through the decade of the 1980s, the anti-abortion movement was in the ascendency as the movement attracted the support of established religious organizations, women's and other groups, and elected politicians. It also led to the formation of new public interest groups, such as Women Abused by Abortion. One commentator suggests that the "powerful, relentless march forward by the pro-life movement has been one of the political phenomena of the eighties" (Woodman 1989: 21). In fact, the anti-abortion movement managed to corner the pro-abortion movement into a position of defensiveness (Woodman 1989). The tactics of groups active in the anti-abortion movement ranged from minor civil disobedience, such as the picketing of abortion clinics (*The Economist* 1989), to the actions of fringe groups in the social movement (Yarnold n.d.), such as Operation Rescue, whose members during the 1980s bombed 32 clinics, set fire to 38, issued death threats to clinic workers, and harassed women at abortion clinics (Woodman 1989; Cockburn 1989).

The anti-abortion coalition had some policy successes in the 1980s, as state and local governments became involved in placing limits on abortion. As earlier mentioned, Republican Presidents Reagan (1980–88) and Bush (elected in 1988) were both committed to an anti-abortion position. Congress made many attempts in the 1980s to weaken the Supreme Court's decision in *Roe v. Wade* (1973), including congressional attempts to eliminate public funding of abortion (Appleton 1981; Horan 1981) and to pass a Human Life Statute or amendment to the U.S. Constitution (Segers 1982).

The efforts of the anti-abortion movement also met with an important judicial victory in the 1989 case of *Webster v. Reproductive Health Services*, which served to severely limit women's access to abortions (Woodman 1989). Specifically, the Supreme Court allowed Missouri, and thus state governments generally, to ban the use of public hospitals and other facilities supported by public funds for the performance of non-therapeutic abortions (those not necessary to save a woman's life). It also upheld the right of Missouri to ban public employees from performing or participating in abortions and substantially increased the costs of an abortion by sanctioning a state law that required doctors to perform a battery of tests after 20 weeks of pregnancy to determine if the fetus could survive outside of the mother's womb (Cockburn 1989).

Anti-abortion groups were temporarily emboldened by the court's decision in *Webster* and engaged in a vigorous campaign to push through state and federal laws restricting abortion (*The Economist* 1989). The *Webster* decision of 1989, however, had the much more significant effect of mobilizing a strong backlash against the anti-abortion lobby (Woodman 1989). Some suggest that the court's ruling in this case galvanized the pro-abortion movement and led to its resurgence at the end of the 1980s (*The Economist* 1989). In fact, on April 9, 1989, 300,000 pro-abortion demonstrators converged on Washington (Woodman 1989). Their efforts were coordinated by groups such as the National Organization for Women (Cockburn 1989). This in turn led to the formation of new pro-abortion groups. Cockburn (1989: 19) describes the new, revitalized pro-abortion movement and its membership:

> The women's movement now vows to create a storm across the country in defence of abortion rights. Pro-choice people who in the past voted their conservative economic interests, never expecting that anything could unhinge abortion rights which they considered established, are now beginning to have second thoughts. The cautiously liberal National Organization for Women is planning to launch nationwide caravans modelled on the civil rights movement's freedom rides and to hold demonstrations that violate the law. Women who have never attended a protest march in their life are travelling to distant cities and filling the streets in their own towns.

The above demonstrates that the abortion issue intimately affects the interests of powerful interest groups in the United States and even led these groups to coalesce into the strong anti-abortion movement of the 1980s, followed by the ascendancy of the pro-abortion movement by 1989. Hence, federal court outcomes in abortion cases are politicized not only due to the fact that abortion is a major issue but also because the litigation issue deeply affects the interests of powerful anti- and pro-abortion groups in the United States.

Lending strong support to this argument is the fact that the only significant political variable in the federal district court abortion cases was the involvement of pro-abortion interest groups in litigation. Other political variables, such as the partisan affiliation of the judges (or their appointing presidents), the preferences of judicial constituents (here defined as politically powerful congresswomen within judges' states), and the involvement of anti-abortion interest groups, did not seem to affect judicial decision making in abortion cases.

On closer inspection of interest group involvement in abortion litigation, one of the most striking observations is the overwhelming involvement of interest groups in the abortion cases considered in this analysis: 66 percent of the abortion cases had interest group involvement. Further, pro-abortion groups enjoyed a 6.5 to 1 advantage over anti-abortion forces in terms of their involvement in these cases and met with considerable litigation success: A pro-abortion decision was entered in 77 percent of the cases. Hence, the involvement of pro-abortion interest groups in litigation seems to have had the effect of fostering lower court implementation of the Supreme Court's ruling in *Roe v. Wade*. It is difficult to assess whether the district courts were responding to the political clout of these groups or to their superior capabilities in litigation (Yarnold 1990a, 1990b, 1991); it was likely a combination of the two.

Previous research (Yarnold 1990b) links litigation success to cooperative litigation efforts by interest groups. In the abortion cases examined, pro-abortion interest groups not only had numerical superiority in terms of appearance in district court cases but also the major advantage of engaging in joint litigation with similar groups that shared their position on the abortion issue.

The pro-abortion position was strengthened through the multiple representation it received in the federal courts, as diverse groups came to advocate the position. For example, pro-abortion arguments were made in these cases by women's groups, groups of health-care providers that have a financial stake in liberal abortion laws, broad-based civil liberties groups, and even, in some instances, by religious organizations. Further, these groups often banded together in abortion cases, engaging in quite effective joint litigation strategies.

In spite of their broader power in U.S. politics, anti-abortion groups shared none of the advantages of pro-abortion groups in litigation before the federal district courts. Specifically, anti-abortion litigation was sporadic (only 10 percent of the cases involved anti-abortion groups, as opposed to 65 percent for the pro-abortion position), did not have the benefit of multiple representation by different groups with similar interests, and showed little evidence of cooperative litigation efforts between anti-abortion groups. Anti-abortion groups tended to make solo appearances, with a small number of groups representing their position. It is not altogether surprising that the federal courts adopted an anti-abortion position in only 23 percent of the cases.

In previous analysis (Yarnold 1990a, 1990b, 1991), I found that region was not significantly related to court outcomes in federal court cases involving claims for political asylum and the withholding of deportation and requests for international extradition. In an attempt to reconcile these findings with previous research that found a relationship between region and judicial outcomes in environmental cases (Wenner 1982; Wenner and Dutter 1988) and race relations cases (Richardson and Vines 1978), it was posited that regional effects might be most apparent in cases that involve a highly ideological issue.

In accordance with this argument, region is significantly related to outcome in the federal court abortion cases examined here. Specifically, the West region is a significant regional variable; cases decided by courts in the West tended to go against the pro-abortion position more often than cases decided by judges in district courts in the Midwest, North, and South.

To find evidence of the highly ideological nature of the abortion issue in the United States, one need look no further than daily press coverage, which chronicles the intensity of the battle between pro- and anti-abortion forces, the effect the abortion issue has had on political campaigns throughout the country, and the massive mobilization of individuals into pro- and anti-abortion movements (*The Economist* 1989).

Instead of passively interpreting the law and the facts of cases, the federal courts in abortion cases were dealing with a major issue that mobilized citizens and interest groups in a battle with a high level of intensity and ideological content. These courts were not immune to their larger political and environmental context but became directly involved in making critical decisions on abortion rights that had the potential of generating intense hostility and controversy.

In the process, the courts responded to a political factor—the involvement of pro-abortion interest groups in litigation—and their regions.

Overall, it must be said that the federal courts did not, in abortion cases, shirk their responsibilities through procedural technicalities (for example, not many cases were dismissed on the basis that litigants lacked standing) but instead actively pursued their policy-making function. These decisions, 77 percent of which adopted a pro-abortion position, served to collectively reinforce the Supreme Court's ruling in *Roe v. Wade*, which recognized the abortion rights of women. The lower federal courts, for the most part, served to foster implementation of the *Roe* decision.

The burden of this federal court policy making was not equally borne by all. The "typical" abortion case was decided in a district court in the Midwest or North and involved pro-abortion interest groups that mounted a successful challenge to a state abortion policy. Federal district courts judges were thus activists when it came to state policy and, through their decisions in abortion cases, whipped law makers and judges in the Midwest and North into conformity with the national norm for abortion that was set forth in *Roe v. Wade* (1973).

II

Judicial versus Administrative Decision Making

4

Comparing Judicial and Administrative Decision Making

CASE STUDY 5: ADJUDICATION BY AGENCIES OR COURTS—DOES THE FORUM MATTER?

A Comparison of Adjudication by the Federal Courts and an Administrative Appeals Board: Asylum-Related Appeals 1980–87

Administrative and judicial decision making are rarely considered together. Analysts tend to treat them separately, as though the two processes have little in common. In some cases, separate treatment is justified. However, in other instances it becomes clear that administrative and judicial decision makers are engaged in similar processes.

For example, it may be appropriate to consider agency and judicial decision making together when both are engaged in adjudication, or the application of the law to individual cases. Comparing administrative and judicial adjudication is particularly appropriate when both types of decision makers must, in order to reach a decision, interpret and apply the same statute. In both instances, the decision maker is confronted with the task of making a legal determination (they usually rely on the factual findings of lower-level decision makers) and, depending on the specificity of the statute in question, may be in a position to exercise a great deal of discretion.

Many analysts have suggested that vague statutes passed by Congress serve to delegate policy-making authority to agencies, which are able to fill in the details by issuing regulations (Simon 1957; Simon, Smithburg, and Thompson 1962; Mazmanian and Sabatier 1983; Lowi 1979; Pious 1979). Agencies interpret vague statutes in such a way as to promote their own policy goals even where these conflict with congressional policy goals (Lipsky 1980; Bardach 1984; Mazmanian and Sabatier 1983). Hence, agencies are not greatly constrained in their rulemaking by the law.

Similarly, the law school model of judicial decision making, which posits that judges impassively apply the law of a case to the facts in order to reach a decision, has been largely discarded, primarily due to the realization that neither the law nor the facts that judges rely upon are objective or knowable (Wenner 1982; Wenner and Dutter 1988; Baum 1989; Frank 1978; Epstein 1985; Yarnold 1990, 1990b, 1991a).

Frank (1978) suggests that the facts on which judges rely resemble guesses, arrived at through an adversarial process in which litigants have great incentive to mold the facts to their advantage. Facts are forgotten or omitted, and litigants may misrepresent the facts. Similarly, the law that judges are to apply is not objective. Statutes that must be construed by judges are (as in the administrative context) vague and contain conflicting policy goals. Previous cases relied on by judges may also be an unreliable guide to the law; it may not be clear whether a previous case is applicable (it may be, for example, distinguishable on the facts), and it may be difficult to identify the holding of a case. Due to the fact that both the law and the facts that apply to a given case are not clear, judges are often left without clear decision rules and must develop their own. Hence, judges do more than simply interpret the law in specific factual disputes. Like administrative decision makers, judges wield a great deal of discretion in their decision making and are properly viewed as policy makers.

This suggests that administrative and judicial decision makers may be relatively unconstrained in their adjudicative decision making by the existence of law, such as statutes. However, this does not suggest that agencies and courts wield their discretion in a similar manner. Traditional legal theory suggests that agencies are often prone to abuse in their decision making due to their status as civil servants, which insulates them from supervisory control, and to the fact that agency clientele often consists of individuals who are not in a position to challenge agency action due to their poverty and low educational levels (Carter 1983; Mashaw 1985). The courts are presumably independent of agencies, and act to correct agency abuses. One does not therefore anticipate that the federal courts, for example, in their consideration of appeals from agency determinations, will perpetuate agency policies that border on abuse, such as decisions that discriminate against certain members of society.

However, when both agencies and courts engage in adjudication, one reasonably expects that similar factors influence judicial and administrative decision making. These common factors may be labeled litigation-related factors.

Many analysts have come to agree that court outcomes very often favor those with superior litigation resources and that organized interests have a disproportionate advantage in litigation. For example, Galanter (1974, 1978) and others (Dolbeare 1978; Epstein 1985; Wenner 1982) suggest that organizations that resort frequently to litigation tend to win cases more often than those who are not repeatedly involved in litigation. Even with a private attorney, the latter do not have the advantages that accrue to individuals involved in litigation on a continuous basis. First, organizations often gain experience and expertise in litigation and have organizational resources such as information that may be used to effectively argue the merits of a case (Vose 1959; O'Connor 1980). Some groups, such as public interest organizations, engage in extensive interaction with other organizations involved in similar types of litigation (Epstein 1985). As a result of informal exchanges of information and more formal cooperative efforts, organizations are able to maximize their resources and effectiveness in litigation. Continuous input by organizations allows them to change the governing rules to their advantage (Galanter 1974, 1978). As a repeat player, the federal government, for example, is quite successful in gaining access to the Supreme Court (Tanenhaus et al. 1981) and in prevailing in subsequent appeals (Tanenhaus 1961; Carrington 1974).

If both agencies and courts are engaged in adjudication, these predictions should also apply to agency adjudications. One expects from the above that court outcomes will tend to favor litigants who are repeat players themselves (such as the federal government and business corporations) or have such players arguing on their behalf (for example, individuals who are either represented by interest groups or have interest groups arguing on their behalf as *amicus curiae*). By the same token, repeat players should also prevail in agency adjudications.

This prediction is based on the assumption that the reason repeat players are so successful in court cases is that they have superior litigation resources that make them particularly able litigants before both agencies and the courts. However, another explanation for the success of repeat players in litigation, and the one argued here, is that these groups are important political actors and that judges are thus responding not as much to their superior arguments on the merits but to their political importance.

The usual retort to this suggestion is that it may apply to elected state court judges but not to their federal counterparts, who are immune to political pressure because they are appointed and not elected. The perception of the federal courts as apolitical has come under increasing attack in recent years (Schubert 1965). Federal court outcomes appear to be related to such political variables as the political party of judges and the partisan affiliation of the president who appointed them (Carp and Rowland 1983). Public opinion is also suggested as a factor that affects federal court outcomes (Cook 1981; Kritzer 1978; Graeber 1973).

In favoring such repeat players as the federal government and interest groups, the federal courts may not therefore be responding so much to their superior arguments as to their political importance.

Although it has been asserted that the federal courts are subject to political influences, insufficient attention has been given to the question of why federal court judges should be subject to those pressures. Baum (1989), in his discussion of the Supreme Court, touches on this question with his suggestion that, prior to their appointment, Supreme Court justices had active political careers. Hence, lower federal court judges (both district and appeals) may be attentive to politically important litigants, such as interest groups (which often lobby for or against judicial candidates during the course of congressional committee hearings and present their views to executive branch officials) and the federal government.

It may be that agencies that engage in adjudication are not subject to the same political pressures as the federal courts. If this is true, one would expect that agency adjudications will not tend to favor politically important litigants such as interest groups and the federal government. Instead, agency officials who engage in adjudication may be influenced by other political pressures that are more related to the internal operations of the agency in question and bear more directly on the ability of these decision makers to gain promotion (and other rewards) within the agency.

This research explores whether agencies and the federal courts are subject to the same political influences in their adjudicative decision making.

Agency versus Federal Court Adjudication in Asylum-Related Appeals

Most immigrants to the United States come for employment or family reunification purposes. However, refugees and political asylees flee their countries because they fear or will likely experience persecution if returned. One main difference between refugees and asylees is that refugees file their applications when they are outside of the United States, while asylees (including applicants for both political asylum and withholding of deportation) file their applications after their arrival in the United States.

The focus here is on asylum policy, which includes decisions relating to both political asylum and withholding of deportation, two mechanisms in U.S. law that allow refugees who are in the United States or at a port of entry to remain if they have a well-founded fear of persecution (in the case of asylum), or if there exists a clear probability of persecution if they are deported (withholding of deportation). Asylum-related cases and appeals involve claims for either asylum or withholding of deportation.

Asylum was first given explicit statutory recognition in 1980, with passage of the Refugee Act of 1980. Section 208(a) of this Act allows refugees within the United States to apply for asylum and sets forth the following definition of a refugee:

[A]ny person who is outside any country of such person's nationality, or in the case of a person having no nationality, is outside any country in which such person last habitually resided, and who is unable to avail himself or herself of the protection of that country because of persecution or a well-founded fear of persecution on account of race, religion, nationality, membership in a particular social group, or political opinion.

There are three routes through which an alien may attempt to obtain political asylum: First, an alien may file an application for asylum with a district office of the Immigration and Naturalization Service if the alien is in the United States and if neither exclusion nor deportation proceedings have been initiated. Second, in the event that this application for asylum is unsuccessful, an alien may, in a subsequent deportation or exclusion proceeding, resubmit the request for asylum to an immigration judge. Third, the alien may request asylum for the first time during the course of an exclusion or deportation hearing.

Appeals may be taken from adverse decisions of immigration judges on asylum applications. If an asylum application is made in the course of a deportation proceeding, and it is denied, administrative review is to the Board of Immigration Appeals, and subsequent judicial review is to the federal courts of appeal. If an application for asylum is raised during the course of an exclusion hearing, and it is denied, administrative review is to the BIA, and subsequent judicial review is through a *habeas corpus* petition to a federal district court. The ruling of the district court on the *habeas corpus* petition may be appealed to the federal courts of appeal.

A limited form of asylum has existed in U.S. law since the passage of the Immigration and Nationality Act of 1952, referred to as "withholding of deportation." Initially, severe restrictions were placed on eligibility for withholding. The 1952 Act established that it was within the attorney general's discretion to choose not to deport aliens who would be subject to physical persecution. Subsequent amendments substantially broadened this provision, and current legislation prohibits the attorney general from deporting an alien who faces a "clear probability" of persecution on account of race, religion, nationality, membership in a particular social group, or political opinion (Section 243(h) of the 1952 Immigration and Nationality Act). Applications for withholding of deportation may be raised in the course of exclusion and deportation hearings (Steel 1985).

Appeals from adverse orders of immigration judges on requests for withholding of deportation follow the same route as appeals in asylum cases.

Hypotheses

In contrast to the traditional model of the judiciary as a passive interpreter of the law, and of agencies as passive policy implementers, federal court judges and members of the BIA were relatively unconstrained in their adjudicative decision making due to the fact that the standards, set forth in the Refugee Act of 1980, that they were called on to interpret are relatively vague. In asylum-related appeals involving claims for withholding, both the courts and the BIA were concerned with whether immigration judges properly found that an alien did or did not face a "clear probability" of persecution. In appeals involving claims for asylum, the applicable standard was a "well-founded fear" of persecution.

Many immigration experts have commented on the ambiguity of these terms, and the apparent arbitrariness of decisions made by both administrative and judicial decision makers when called on to interpret these standards. Blum (1986) suggests, for example, that these standards do not suggest to an alien how much and what kind of evidence he or she is required to provide or what criteria the trier of fact and the reviewing body should use in analyzing the evidence. Edwards (1983) concludes that the standards contain both objective and subjective elements, and that it is difficult to determine the meaning of either standard. Hyndman (1986) adds that ambiguity is added to the analysis since there is no commonly accepted definition of the core requirement—persecution—for both asylum and withholding claims.

It should come as no surprise, given the vagueness of the underlying standards for asylum and withholding, that administrative and judicial decisions on both types of claims have been attacked as arbitrary. The vagueness of the underlying statute gives great discretion to these decision makers.

*Decision Making by the BIA: Bias in Favor of Aliens
from Hostile Countries*

In spite of its humanitarian guise, U.S. refugee and asylum policy, since World War II and the emergence of the Cold War, has been consistently biased in favor of aliens from "hostile" states. This bias was introduced in the course of a propaganda war with the Soviet Union on the assumption that the presence of hostile-country aliens in the United States would attest to the intolerable conditions to which they were previously subjected, thus embarrassing their former governments and simultaneously providing evidence of U.S. generosity and compassion. This hostile-country bias was one of the motivating forces behind the Refugee Act of 1980, which replaced standards favoring communist countries for refugee admissions with non-ideological standards.

In spite of passage of the Refugee Act of 1980, administrative agencies responsible for implementing the Act (including the INS, immigration judges, and consular offices within the Department of State) continue to favor aliens from hostile countries of origin (Yarnold 1990b).

Helton (1984), for example, suggests that although claims are ostensibly subject to an objective standard, many applicants for asylum and withholding are turned down for reasons relating to U.S. foreign policy. Thus, for example, the government often labels Haitians escaping the Duvalier regime and Salvadoran and Guatemalan refugees as "economic" and not political refugees. Parker (1985) asserts that efforts to secure asylum for Salvadorans and Guatemalans have led only to a "blind alley." Salvadorans and Guatemalans are routinely repatriated, in spite of the fact that they are fleeing ongoing civil strife.

In 1984, the INS processed the asylum applications of over 13,000 Salvadorans and rejected 97.5 percent of them. This rate contrasts sharply with the average approval rate of asylum applications of 30 percent for that year. Van Der Hout (1985:1) comments: "If you're a Russian ballerina, a Romanian gymnast or a Chinese tennis player, your road to asylum is quick and easy." He notes further that Nicaraguans fleeing from "socialism" are also subject to preferential treatment; their approval rate for asylum claims was five times higher in 1984 than was the approval rate for Salvadorans.

Helton (1984) agrees that U.S. foreign policy considerations have dominated and continue to dominate its asylum and refugee policy. For example, the attorney general's parole authority, which allows persons to enter the United States "for emergent reasons or for reasons deemed strictly in the public interest" is, on its face, a neutral standard. Nevertheless, Helton (1984) indicates that admissions made under this provision for the period 1956–67 favored aliens from hostile countries.

Even after the United States became a party to the United Nations Protocol Relating to the Status of Refugees, and thereby agreed to adhere to a neutral standard for refugee admissions, foreign policy considerations continued to dominate refugee admissions. In the period 1968–80, prior to passage of the Refugee Act of 1980, Helton (1984) claims, the parole authority of the attorney general primarily benefitted aliens from hostile countries.

Helton (1984:250) asserts that the Refugee Act of 1980 "established a standard for uniform and nonideological refugee eligibility. Congress intended this new standard to be compatible with the humanitarian traditions and international obligations of the United States." In spite of these policy goals, Helton claims that U.S. asylum and refugee policy after 1980 continues to be biased in favor of hostile-country aliens.

There is much support for the proposition that U.S. foreign policy considerations dominate its refugee and asylum policy even after passage of the Refugee Act of 1980 (Yarnold 1988; 1990b). However, a question remains as to how these foreign policy objectives are communicated to decision makers within the immigration bureaucracy. Loescher and Scanlan (1986) suggest that U.S. foreign policy objectives are communicated through State Department advisory opinions in cases involving claims for asylum and withholding of deportation; these opinions are issued by the Bureau of Human Rights and Humanitarian Affairs (BHRHA). Preston (1986) notes also the significant role given to State Department advisory opinions in asylum applications. For each application, before an INS agent may determine if an alien is eligible for asylum, the application must first be forwarded to the State Department for an advisory opinion that is often dispositive of asylum-related applications because adjudicating officers tend to give great deference to the opinion and rarely rule against its conclusions.

There are several reasons to predict that the BIA, as a part of the immigration bureaucracy, will perpetuate the bias of lower-level administrative officials in favor of hostile-country aliens. The first is a procedural one: The BIA most often relies on the findings made by lower-level administrative decision makers who, in turn, give great deference to State Department advisory opinions that favor applicants from hostile countries. Hence, the BIA, as an appeals board, tends to be an affirming body. A second reason relates to the composition of the BIA, whose members have often had careers in the immigration bureaucracy prior to their appointment and have thus been socialized into standard agency routines and decision-making processes.

Decision Making by the Federal Courts: Bias in Favor of Organizational Litigants

One does not expect that the federal courts, like administrative decision makers below, will favor in asylum-related appeals aliens from hostile countries of origin. The federal courts are, after all, independent of the immigration bureaucracy and are expected to correct abuses by administrative decision makers.

Instead, the federal courts, in accordance with the earlier discussion, may decide asylum-related appeals in favor of aliens who have organizations appearing on their behalf either in a representative capacity or as *amicus curiae*.

One may base this prediction on the following. First, such organizations are repeat players in litigation and have superior litigation resources that enable them to effectively argue the merits of a case. Since the opponent in this case is the federal government, another repeat player, the presence of an organization on an alien's behalf tends to make the alien's odds a little more favorable. Second, judges will more often decide asylum-related appeals in favor of aliens when interest groups are involved on the aliens' behalf because of the political importance of interest groups, which may lobby in favor of (or oppose) the promotion of judges within the ranks of the federal judiciary.

If the organizational advantage in appeals is, as argued earlier, primarily due to the superior litigation resources of organizations, one would expect that organizations will enjoy the same advantages in administrative appeals to the BIA.

If, however, as predicted, federal court judges are responding primarily to the political significance of interest groups, one does not expect that the BIA will be similarly influenced. Instead, organizational involvement should not be significantly related to decisions that favor aliens.

Control Variables

Other analysts suggest that contextual variables are significantly related to judicial and administrative decision making (Dye 1966; Hofferbert 1974). Regional variances, for example, appear to be related to judicial outcomes (Wenner 1982; Wenner and Dutter 1988; Vines 1963; Giles and Walker 1978; Carp and Rowland 1983). Economists also assert that U.S. refugee policy, as a subgroup of general U.S. immigration policy, is influenced by economic conditions in the United States, particularly the unemployment rate (Briggs 1984; Loescher and Scanlan

1986; Chiswick 1981, 1986). Hence, a competing hypothesis is that administrative and federal court outcomes in asylum-related appeals are significantly related to the unemployment rate in the United States shortly prior to the time that the appeals were decided.

Critics of U.S. refugee and asylum policy also maintain that it is biased in favor of aliens from European countries (Loescher and Scanlan 1986; Preston 1986). This variable is included as a second control variable.

Data and Methods

Data employed for the analysis of BIA decision making consist of 27 published decisions of the BIA for the period of January 1, 1980, to July 1987 in which litigants raised asylum-related issues on appeal, and a random sample of 360 unpublished decisions of the BIA in asylum-related appeals for the period of January 1, 1980, to July 1987. The unpublished decisions were obtained by visiting BIA headquarters in Falls Church, Virginia. From 1980 to 1987, there were approximately 20,000 unpublished BIA decisions; 10 percent of these appeals raised the issue of asylum and/or withholding. These decisions are stored alphabetically in binders and divided into six-month periods. A random sample of these volumes was taken by examining only certain letters of the alphabet for each six-month period. Only those unpublished decisions of the BIA that involved asylum and/or withholding were examined; the 360 asylum-related appeals constitute about 18 percent of all such appeals. The published and unpublished decisions of the BIA in asylum-related appeals were added together for a total data set of 387 appeals.

Data for federal court decision making consist of all decisions in asylum-related appeals published in official reporters for the federal district courts (*Federal Supplement*) and federal courts of appeal (*Federal Reporter*) for the period of January 1, 1980, to September 1, 1987. There were 146 asylum-related appeals.

This analysis examines the extent to which decisions on asylum-related appeals may be explained by the following independent variables: the involvement of interest groups in the appeal; the unemployment rate; whether the alien was from a hostile country of origin; and whether the alien was European. There are two equations, one for asylum-related appeals to the BIA and another for asylum-related appeals to the federal courts.

The dependent variable is dichotomous, which makes standard regression analysis inappropriate, because regression assumes that the dependent variable is continuous. The dependent variable is whether an alien or aliens involved in an asylum-related appeal to the BIA or the federal courts won the appeal.

The participation of interest groups is measured by examining written opinions for each of the BIA and federal court decisions in asylum-related appeals. These written decisions list all of the litigants involved and their representatives. Another part of the analysis involving interest groups consisted of combining all of the BIA and federal court appeals (a total of 533). A list was compiled of all of these groups (listed in Appendix A); 60 organizational litigants were identified. Subsequently, these organizations were interviewed, using the Organization Information Sheet contained in Appendix B.

The unemployment rate was measured for six months prior to the month in which a decision was rendered. For district courts, the unemployment rate was taken for the city in which a district court judge sits. For courts of appeals, since these courts generally consist of a panel of three judges, the unemployment rate was calculated by taking the average unemployment rate for the six-month period in the three cities in which judges sit (U.S. Department of Labor, 1980–87).

For BIA appeals, the average national unemployment rate was examined during a six-month period preceding the month in which the BIA rendered a decision in a appeal (U.S. Department of Labor, 1980–87). The unemployment rate for both federal court and BIA appeals has been dichotomized at its mean.

In most appeals, the country of origin of the alien is listed. To determine whether countries of origin are "hostile" to the United States, since this determination is most often made by the State Department, background notes published by the State Department's Bureau of Public Affairs were consulted. (U.S. Department of State, 1980–87). When background notes label countries as communist, socialist, or leftist, these countries are labeled "hostile." As seen in Appendix C, 71 of 387 asylum-related appeals to the BIA involved aliens from hostile states; thus, approximately 18 percent of all BIA appeals involve hostile-state aliens. As seen in Appendix D, of 145 asylum-related appeals to the federal courts, 20 percent (n = 30) involve aliens from hostile countries. These figures contrast with the percentage of applications filed with the INS (1983–85, asylum applications) and the State Department (1982–85, refugee applications) in recent years. From Appendix E, of a total of 70,815 asylum applications filed, 43,874, or roughly 62 percent, involve aliens from hostile states. Similarly, of a total of 342,388 refugee applications filed during this period, 335,930, or about 99 percent, were filed by hostile-state aliens.

The drop-off in appeals by hostile-state aliens to the BIA (to 18 percent of the total) and to the federal courts (20 percent of total) may be attributed to the high success rates enjoyed by hostile-state applicants for asylum and refugee status from the INS and State Department. In the period 1983–85, hostile-state aliens had their asylum claims approved 33 percent of the time, when the mean approval rate was 13 percent, and the success rate for non-hostile-state aliens was only 4 percent (Yarnold 1988, 1990b). Similarly, hostile-state aliens who claimed refugee status were approved 80 percent of the time, while non-hostile-state aliens were approved 78 percent of the time (a statistically significant difference due to the large size of the sample); the mean approval rate for refugee applications was 43 percent (Yarnold 1988, 1990b).

From the State Department's background notes, it is also possible to determine whether the countries of origin of aliens involved in the appeal are European. Consulting again Appendix C, one observes that 10 of the 387 appeals involve aliens from European countries, which is about 2 percent of the total. For federal court appeals (Appendix D), approximately 3 percent of the appeals involve aliens from Europe (n = 5).

There is also a drop-off in the presence of Europeans at the appeals level. Of 70,815 asylum applications filed with the INS from 1983 to 1985, 6,517 involved aliens from Europe, which is about 9 percent of the total. Europeans were 12 percent more likely than non-Europeans to have their asylum applications approved by the INS (Yarnold 1988, 1990b).

Statistical analysis consists of probit analysis because the dependent variable, whether aliens prevail in asylum-related appeals to the BIA or the federal courts, is dichotomous and there are multiple independent variables. When dealing with a dependent variable that is ordinal, prior analysts have used probit analysis, or multivariate probability unit, instead of regression, which assumes that a dependent variable is measured at an interval level (Aldrich and Cnudde 1975; Segal 1984; Pindyck and Rubinfeld 1981; Wenner and Dutter 1988). Parameter estimates are obtained in probit analysis through the maximum likelihood estimation (MLE) method, which assumes that the error term is normally distributed. MLE estimates are made for each independent variable included in the model and represent the amount of change produced in the cumulative normal probability function by a one unit change in an independent variable (Segal 1984). MLEs are calculated for each independent variable, as are the standard errors of the MLEs. The MLEs divided by their standard errors approximate a normal distribution (Segal 1984). Hence it is possible to test whether individual independent variables are statistically significant, when controlling for the effects of other independent variables. Where there are predictions about the direction of individual estimates, as is true here, one-tail tests are employed (Wenner and Dutter 1988).

Aldrich and Cnudde (1975) have suggested that the F of observed least square (OLS) regression, which tests the overall significance of a model has an analog in probit analysis: –2 times the log of the likelihood ratio, which (in large samples) is a chi-square statistic, with degrees of freedom equal to the number of independent variables. This analog is described as "a comparison of the probability of observing this sample if the MLE estimates are correct . . . to the situation if all coefficients were zero (i.e., the null model)" (Aldrich and Cnudde 1975: 601).

The goodness of fit of a model is measured through an R2, as in OLS regression (Segal 1984), and through an examination of the chi-square statistic calculated for an equation divided by its degree of freedom (d.f.). Finally, it is possible to measure how well a model performs in predicting the outcome for the data employed in an analysis through a measure of the percentage that is predicted correctly (Segal 1984; Wenner and Dutter 1988; Yarnold 1988, 1990a, 1990b, 1990c).

Findings

Tables 4.1 and 4.2 contain the results of probit analysis for BIA and federal court decision making in asylum-related appeals.

Table 4.1
Probit Estimates for BIA Determinations in Asylum-Related Appeals, 1980–87

Dependent Variable: Did Alien Win Asylum-Related Appeal

Variable	Maximum Likelihood Estimate (MLE)	Standard Error (SE)	MLE/SE
Constant	-1.38	0.13	-10.30 *
Organizational Participation	0.89	0.76	1.17
Hostile State Of Origin	1.45	0.60	2.40 *
High Unemployment Rate	0.93	0.67	1.39
European State Of Origin	-0.25	1.95	-0.13

Chi-Square = 12.66   DF = 4   P = 0.08
N = 387
*Significant at 0.05

As predicted, the only significant independent variable in the equation for BIA decision making is whether the alien was from a country hostile to the United States. Aliens from countries hostile to the United States were more likely to prevail in asylum-related appeals to the BIA than were aliens from non-hostile countries. Not significantly related to outcome was organizational participation in the appeal, the unemployment rate, and whether the alien was from a European country of origin.

The only significant independent variable in the equation for federal court decision making is whether there was organizational involvement in the appeal. Aliens who were represented by organizations or had organizations appearing as *amicus curiae* and arguing in their favor were more likely to prevail in their asylum-related appeals to the federal courts than were aliens without organizational involvement. Unrelated to federal court decision making in these appeals was whether the alien was from a hostile country of origin, whether the alien was from Europe, and the unemployment rate.

Interviews were conducted for 57 of the 60 organizations that were involved in asylum-related appeals to the BIA and the federal courts, either as representatives of aliens or as *amicus curiae*. One of the organizations is a labor organization; 56, or 98 percent, are legal services organizations. There were no business or ethnic organizations involved in these appeals.

These legal service organizations are located throughout the United States and provide legal services to aliens, including assistance with their claims for asylum and withholding. They do not, by and large, rely on membership fees as a source of support. Appendix E lists their sources of support, which include private foundations, state government, religious organizations, the federal government,

Table 4.2
Probit Estimates for Federal District and Court of Appeals Determinations in Asylum-Related Appeals, 1980–87

Dependent Variable: Did Alien Win Asylum-Related Appeal

Variable	Maximum Likelihood Estimate (MLE)	Standard Error (SE)	MLE/SE
Constant	-1.28	0.36	-3.58 *
Organizational Participation	2.44	0.77	3.17 *
Hostile State Of Origin	-0.30	0.74	-0.39
High Unemployment Rate	-0.58	0.73	-0.79
European State Of Origin	0.05	1.82	0.03

Chi-Square = 13.26   DF = 4   P = 0.07
N = 145
*Significant at 0.05

bar organizations, individual donors, law schools and law school alumni, local government, the sale of publications, law firm donations, nominal fees charged for representation, other public interest organizations, and corporations. Ninety-five percent of the legal services organizations (53 of 56) rely on non-membership sources of support; only three (or 5 percent) of the legal services organizations indicated that they rely exclusively on membership dues as a source of support.

Over three-quarters of the legal services organizations were formed since 1970, which suggests these organizations are a relatively recent phenomenon. Seventy percent of these organizations require that clients fall below the poverty line; 73 percent of these groups charge no fee for their services, while 27 percent collect nominal fees.

These organizations vary greatly in terms of their staffing and budgetary resources. Most have paid attorneys on their staffs, and few rely exclusively on the services of volunteer attorneys. The staff size of these organizations ranges from a low of one to a high of 155; their mean staff size is 17 persons. Their annual budgets run from $5,000 to $1,193,190.

Of 55 legal services organizations responding, 82 percent assist aliens in applying for asylum with the INS; 87 percent also assist aliens in deportation and exclusion proceedings hearings before immigration judges. Eighty-six percent represent aliens in asylum-related appeals to the BIA, and 91 percent become involved in asylum-related appeals to the federal courts.

When asked whey they assist aliens, over two-thirds (69%) of the legal services organizations responded that they have no other goal than to assist aliens; 15

percent of these organizations suggest that they are motivated by a desire to affect legal precedent and tend to preselect cases for this purpose. Another 16 percent of the organizations say that they are interested both in helping aliens and affecting legal precedent.

An interesting finding is that 88 percent of the organizational representatives interviewed say that they are aware of the bias of the immigration bureaucracy in favor of aliens from hostile countries. In spite of this, the spokesmen indicated that they remain committed to trying to help aliens through legal channels.

Almost all (90 percent) of the legal services organizations engage in cooperative efforts with other organizations that provide legal services to aliens; 89 percent of these groups share information with other legal services providers, 87 percent send representatives to conferences attended by other legal services providers, and 66 percent engage in joint litigation with similar groups.

The preferred litigation strategy of the legal services organizations is to appear as representatives of aliens; 56 percent appear in a representative capacity, 11 percent appear only as *amicus curiae*, and 33 percent pursue a mixed litigation strategy.

Discussion

The BIA, an administrative entity within the immigration bureaucracy, and the federal courts (district and appeals) had conflicting policy goals in their decision making on asylum-related appeals during the period 1980–87. Although U.S. refugee and asylum policy is ostensibly humanitarian and subject to a neutral standard, the BIA served to reinforce the pro-hostile-country bias of lower-level decision makers within the immigration bureaucracy, including the INS, immigration judges, and the State Department. The effect of this bias is that aliens from communist, socialist, and leftist countries of origin are more likely to prevail in asylum-related appeals to the BIA than are aliens from non-hostile countries. The humanitarian goals of U.S. asylum policy are thus subordinated to foreign policy considerations.

The federal courts did not serve to perpetuate the hostile-country bias of the immigration bureaucracy in their decision making on asylum-related appeals. However, federal court judges seem to be influenced in their decision making on these appeals by the involvement of organizations in litigation. Aliens with organizational involvement in their appeals were more likely to prevail than were aliens who lacked organizational support.

One rather striking finding, particularly in light of Olson's (1971) prediction that public interest organizations will fail to organize and maintain themselves due to the "free-rider" problem, is that 98 percent of the organizational participants in these appeals are public interest organizations. Only one, a labor organization, does not fall into this category. A total of 16 percent of the asylum-related appeals to the BIA had organizational involvement; the percentage for federal court appeals is somewhat higher, at 42 percent.

Private interest groups are those that seek to benefit only group members. The labor organization that became involved in one asylum-related appeal was a private interest group, seeking to help a labor union member. In contrast, the legal services organizations that dominated these appeals are public interest organizations. They sought to make a collective benefit—free or low-cost legal representation—available to non-group members, or aliens who applied for asylum and withholding (Yarnold 1988, 1990b).

Walker (1983) and McFarland (1987) suggest that public interest organizations, as one type of large group, have overcome Olson's (1971) free-rider barriers to large group formation and maintenance through relying on interest group patrons, both public and private, in addition to or as a substitute for funds derived from membership dues.

Almost all (95 percent) of the 56 public interest organizations involved in asylum-related appeals to the BIA and the federal courts rely for their support upon non-membership sources. The most important non-membership sources of support for the public interest groups are private foundations, state and federal government, and religious organizations.

How does one account for the fact that these legal public interest groups are, for the most part, a relatively recent phenomenon, most having formed since 1970? A traditional response would suggest that public interest groups gained impetus after the Civil Rights movement of the late 1950s and early 1960s demonstrated the efficacy of organizing in the public interest. The explanation offered here is quite different. It is hypothesized that the catalysts to the formation of the legal public interest groups that assist aliens in asylum-related appeals are previously documented "state interests" (Krasner 1978; Goldstein 1986) in limiting the flow of immigrants to the United States, and favoring in refugee and asylum admissions aliens from hostile countries of origin (Yarnold 1988, 1990b).

In spite of legislation in this area, such as the Refugee Act of 1980, which liberalized refugee and asylum admissions and eliminated the bias in favor of hostile-state aliens, the immigration bureaucracy, consisting of the State Department, the INS, immigration judges, and the BIA, continues to promote both "state interests" in its post-1980 decision making on asylum and refugee claims. Thus, state interests in limiting immigration flows and favoring hostile-state aliens led to a countermobilization of interest groups, such as the ones examined here, that seek to protect the interests of immigrants and, more specifically, refugees and asylees.

Representatives of almost all of the public interest legal groups indicated that they are aware of the hostile-state bias of the immigration bureaucracy in its disposition of asylum and withholding claims and appeals.

Most of the public interest groups that became involved in asylum-related appeals to the BIA and the federal courts pursued these appeals for the purpose of helping the alien involved, rather than to influence legal precedent. The main litigation strategy of these organizations is the direct representation of aliens, rather than appearances as *amicus curiae*.

Most important in explaining the high level of success enjoyed by these organizations in asylum-related appeals to the federal courts is the high level of cooperation of these public interest organizations with other such groups. These public interest organizations regularly exchange information with other public interest groups, attend or sponsor seminars attended by the representatives of similar groups, and engage in joint litigation when the opportunity arises. Perhaps their high success level is also partially attributable to the relative youth of these groups, which enables them to draw on the resources of enthusiastic and motivated staff members, while simultaneously enjoying the usual benefits of litigants who are repeat players.

Hence, one possibility is that aliens with organizational involvement in their asylum-related appeals to the federal courts were more successful than aliens without such involvement because of the superior litigation resources of these groups.

However, here arises an apparent contradiction: If superior organizational resources carried the day in the federal courts, why is it that decision makers on the BIA were not similarly impressed? In asylum-related appeals to the BIA, aliens with organizational involvement fared no better than aliens without the involvement of organizations. One possibility is that the BIA is simply an affirming body, which tends to go along with decisions made by lower-level administrators in the immigration bureaucracy. However, another possibility alluded to earlier is that federal court judges, in favoring litigants linked to organizations, may have responded to the political importance of the interest groups, and not only to their superior litigation resources.

One of the organizations that repeatedly became involved in these appeals was the American Civil Liberties Union. This national organization has offices throughout the United States and seeks to protect civil liberties. In addition to lobbying and advocacy, local affiliates of the ACLU become involved in cases in which aliens claim entitlement to either political asylum or withholding of deportation. The national office of the ACLU in New York City was involved in four asylum-related appeals to the BIA and federal courts in the asylum-related appeals examined in this analysis; the ACLU of Florida also participated in four appeals; the ACLU of Southern California was involved in one appeal; and the ACLU of the national capital area participated in two appeals. The ACLU was therefore involved in 11 of the 533 appeals examined, or roughly 2 percent of these cases. This is rather significant involvement by the ACLU in BIA and federal court adjudication, particularly in view of the ACLU's involvement in other policy areas, such as criminal rights. If nothing else, the presence of the ACLU in federal court adjudication reminds the judiciary both of the political importance of this group and its position on various issues.

Baum (1989) suggests that the ACLU worked to defeat the nomination of William H. Rehnquist to the Supreme Court in 1971 due to his lack of support for civil liberties, and suggests that interest groups play an important role generally in the appointment of Supreme Court justices through their testimony at congressional hearings and lobbying directed at executive branch officials.

Hence, federal court judges, particularly in the lower federal courts (since they may still be promoted within the ranks of the federal judiciary) may be quite attentive to the political power of interest groups that appear before them, with the result that litigants who have organizational involvement in their cases will more often prevail than litigants who do not have organizations arguing on their behalf.

Examples of other public interest organizations involved in asylum-related appeals include Amnesty International, the American Immigration Lawyers' Association, Catholic Community Services, and the Haitian Refugee Center.

Hence, while the federal courts tended to favor aliens who had organizational involvement in their asylum-related appeals, due to the superior litigation resources of these organizations or their political clout, the BIA was not similarly influenced by organizational involvement in asylum-related appeals but served instead to perpetuate the hostile-country bias of the immigration bureaucracy.

Appendix A

List Of Organizations Which Were Involved In Asylum-Related Appeals to the BIA and the Federal Courts as Representatives of Aliens or as Amicus Curiae: 1980 - 1987

Public Interest Organizations Which Participated In Interview:

Mean Wins: 52%

Group	Inputs	Success Rate
American Civil Liberties Union (New York)	4	50%
American Civil Liberties Union of Florida (Coral Gables)	4	50%
American Civil Liberties Union of Southern California (Los Angeles)	1	100%
American Civil Liberties Union of the National Capital Area (D.C.)	2	50%
American Friends Service Committee (Miami, Florida)	1	0%
American Immigration Lawyer's Association (Miami, Florida)	1	0%
Amnesty International, U.S.A. (San Francisco, California)	1	0%
Apostolic Mission of Christ (Miami, Florida)	2	50%
Atlanta Legal Aid Society (Atlanta, Georgia)	10	60%
California Rural Legal Assistance Foundation (El Centro, California)	5	80%
Catholic Community Services (Newark, New Jersey)	1	0%
Catholic Migration and Refugee Office of the Diocese of Brooklyn (New York)	1	0%
Catholic Social Services Immigration Project (San Francisco, California)	1	100%
Central American Refugee Project (Phoenix, Arizona)	1	0%
Centro Asuntos Migratorios (El Centro, California)	7	86%
Centro Para Immigrantes De Houston, Inc. (Houston, Texas)	1	0%
Colorado Rural Legal Services, Inc. (Denver, Colorado)	1	100%
Columbia School of Law Immigration Law Clinic (New York)	2	0%

Public Interest Organizations Which Participated In Interview (cont'):

Group	Inputs	Success Rate
Delaware County Legal Assistance Association (Chester, Pennsylvania)	1	100%
Ecumenical Immigration Services, Inc. (New Orleans, Louisiana)	1	0%
El Concilio Manzo, Inc. (Tucson, Arizona)	6	0%
Florida Institutional Legal Services (Gainesville, Florida)	1	0%
Florida Rural Legal Services, Inc. (West Palm Beach, Florida)	2	100%
George Washington University Immigration Law Clinic (D.C.)	4	25%
Haitian Refugee Center (Miami, Florida)	25	20%
Haitian Refugee Volunteer Task Force of the Dade County Bar Association (Dade County, Florida)	1	100%
Immigrants' Rights Office of the Legal Aid Foundation of Los Angeles (Los Angeles, California)	2	50%
Immigration Law Clinic (Davis, California)	1	100%
Imperial Valley Immigration Law Project (El Centro, California)	9	67%
International Human Rights Law Group (D.C.)	2	50%
International Institute East Bay (Oakland, California)	1	0%
Kansas Legal Services Inc. (Topeka, Kansas)	4	50%
King County Bar Association (Seattle, Washington)	2	50%
L.A. Center for Law and Justice: Immigrants' Rights Defense Project of the International Institute of Los Angeles (California)	1	100%
Lawyers' Committee for Human Rights (New York)	7	28%
Lawyers Guild--Southern California Chapter (Downey, California)	1	100%
Legal Aid Society of Palm Beach (West Palm Beach, Florida)	2	0%
Legal Services Center, Inc. (Jamaica Plain, Massachusetts)	1	0%
Legal Services of Greater Miami, Inc. (Miami, Florida)	2	50%
Loyola Law School Clinic (New Orleans, Louisiana)	1	0%
Lutheran Ministries of Florida (Miami, Florida)	3	0%
Massachusetts Civil Liberties Union (Boston)	1	0%
National Center for Immigrants' Rights (Los Angeles)	3	100%
National Council of Churches (New York)	1	100%
National Emergency Civil Liberties Foundation (New York)	5	60%
National Refugee Rights Project--San Francisco Lawyers' Committee for Urban Affairs (San Francisco)	1	100%
New York Civil Liberties Union (New York)	1	0%
New York University Immigration Law Clinic (New York)	4	0%
Proyecto Libertad (Harlingen Texas)	2	50%
Southern Arizona Legal Aid, Inc. (Tucson, Arizona)	1	0%
Texas Rural Legal Aid (Welasco, Texas)	1	100%
United States Catholic Conference (El Paso, Texas)	2	0%
United States Catholic Conference Migration and Refugee Services (New York)	1	100%
United States Helsinki Watch Committee (New York)	1	100%

Public Interest Organizations Which Participated In Interview (cont'):

Group	Inputs	Success Rate
Washington Lawyers' Committee for Civil Rights Under Law (D.C.)	2	50%
Wyandotte-Leavenworth County Legal Aid Society, Inc. (Kansas City, Ka	2	0%

Public Interest Groups Which Were Not Interviewed:

Group	Inputs	Success Rate
Brooklyn Legal Services (Brooklyn, New York)	4	0%
Comite N.S. Laredo (Brooklyn, New York)	1	0%
International Institute of San Francisco (California)	1	0%

Labor Organizations:

Group	Inputs	Success Rate
Hotel and Restaurant Employees Union Local 25 (D.C.)	3	67%

Appendix B

Organization Information Sheet

1. Identification

      a. year organized
      b. is organization a public interest group? If not,
         what type of group is it? (labor, ethnic, business)

2. Nature of Clients

      a. ethnic/racial background
      b. is fee charged for services?
      c. if fee is charged, is it nominal?
      d. is poverty criterion employed for clients?

3. Contact Person/Date

4. Annual Budget of Organization

5. Source of Funds

6. Staff Size

      a. how many paid staff persons?
      b. does the group use volunteers?

7. Tasks of Organization

      a. does organization help aliens with asylum-related
        claims with:
            --INS
            --immigration judges (exclusion/deportation hearing)
            --BIA (asylum-related appeals)
            --federal courts (asylum-related appeals)
      b. does organization engage in non-legal activities?

8. Goals of Organization

when group becomes involved in asylum-related appeal to the
BIA and the federal courts, is its primary purpose to:
     a. help alien?
     b. affect legal precedent?
     c. both?

9. Bias In Immigration Bureaucracy

Is representative aware of bias in immigration
bureaucracy's asylum-related decision making in
favor of aliens from hostile (communist, socialist,
leftist) countries of origin?

10. Caseload

11. Litigation Strategy of Organization

which litigation strategy is employed:

     a. direct representation of aliens?
     b. appearances as amicus curiae?
     c. combination of the two?

12. Cooperation With Other Organizations

Does the group cooperate with other similar groups
through:
     a. informal exchanges of information?
     b. attending/hosting seminars?
     c. joint litigation?

13. Does Organization Support Sanctuary Movement?

14. Was Group Involved In/Influenced By Sanctuary Movement?

15. General Comments

Appendix C

Percentage Of Asylum-Related Appeals To The BIA
Won By Aliens Of Particular States 1980 - 1987

Number of States: 36
Number of Appeals: 387
Average Wins By Aliens: 12%
n = 387

State	Hostile	Europe	No. Cases	% Wins
Afghanistan	Yes	No	4	50%
Argentina	No	No	1	0%
Bangladesh	No	No	2	0%
Belize	No	No	1	0%
Brazil	No	No	1	0%
Chile	No	No	1	0%
China	Yes	No	18	11%
Costa Rica	No	No	1	0%
Cuba	No	No	97	6%
Dominican Republic	No	No	1	0%
El Salvador	No	No	53	8%
Ethiopia	Yes	No	3	33%
Greece	No	Yes	2	0%
Guatemala	No	No	6	17%
Guyana	No	No	1	0%
Haiti	No	No	89	7%
Honduras	No	No	1	0%
Hong Kong	No	No	1	0%
India	No	No	15	7%
Iran	Yes	No	26	31%
Iraq	No	No	8	0%
Ireland	No	Yes	1	0%
Israel	No	No	1	0%
Lebanon	No	No	1	0%
Liberia	No	No	1	0%
Mexico	No	No	1	0%
Nicaragua	Yes	No	13	23%
Nigeria	No	No	2	0%
Pakistan	No	No	3	0%
Philippines	No	No	5	20%
Poland	Yes	Yes	2	0%
Romania	Yes	Yes	1	100%
Sri Lanka	No	No	1	0%
Taiwan	No	No	2	50%
Turkey	No	No	1	0%
Yugoslavia	Yes	Yes	4	25%

Appendix D

Percentage Of Wins In Asylum-Related Appeals To The Federal
Courts By Aliens Of Different Countries: 1980 - 1987

Number Of Appeals: 145
Number Of Countries: 27
Mean Wins By Aliens: 42%
n = 145

STATE	Hostile	European	No. Cases	% Wins
Afghanistan	Yes	No	1	0%
Austria	No	Yes	1	0%
Chile	No	No	2	50%
China	Yes	No	2	50%
Cuba	No	No	17	53%
Dominica	No	No	1	0%
El Salvador	No	No	39	54%
Ethiopia	Yes	No	1	0%
Ghana	No	No	2	100%
Guatemala	No	No	4	25%
Haiti	No	No	16	44%
India	No	No	1	0%
Iran	Yes	No	19	32%
Iraq	No	No	12	8%
Ireland	No	Yes	2	50%
Mexico	No	No	1	0%
Nicaragua	Yes	No	4	50%
Nigeria	No	No	3	100%
Pakistan	No	No	1	0%
Paraguay	No	No	1	0%
Philippines	No	No	7	57%
Sweden	No	Yes	1	0%
Syria	Yes	No	2	0%
Tonga	No	No	1	0%
Venezuela	No	No	1	0%
Yemen	No	No	2	0%
Yugoslavia	Yes	Yes	1	100%

Appendix E

Tables For INS/State Department Asylum And
Refugee Determinations: 1982 - 1985

Table 1
Asylum Admissions INS (1983 - 1985)

KEY: State Of Origin   1 For Hostile, 0 For Non-Hostile
             Europe   1 For European State, 0 For Non-European

Mean Approvals: 13.05%

STATE	Appeal Approved	Appeal Denied	State of Origin	Europe	% Win
AFGHANISTAN	296	504	1	0	37.00
ALBANIA	0	1	1	0	0.00
ALGERIA	0	5	0	0	0.00
ANGOLA	4	12	1	0	25.00
ANTIGUA-BARBUDA	0	3	0	0	0.00
ARGENTINA	2	104	0	0	1.89
AUSTRALIA	0	0	0	1	-
BAHAMAS	0	3	0	0	0.00
BAHRAIN	0	1	0	0	0.00
BANGLADESH	0	391	0	0	0.00
BELGIUM	0	4	0	1	0.00
BELIZE	0	3	0	0	0.00
BOLIVIA	0	16	0	0	0.00
BOTSWANA	0	1	0	0	0.00
BRAZIL	2	4	0	0	33.33
BULGARIA	20	27	1	1	42.55
BURMA	1	7	0	0	12.50
BURUNDI	0	2	0	0	0.00
CAMEROON	1	4	0	0	20.00
CANADA	0	0	0	1	0.00
CAMBODIA	3	4	1	1	42.86

Table 1 (cont')
Asylum Admissions Ins (1983 - 1985)

STATE	Appeal Approved	Appeal Denied	State of Origin	Europe	% Win
CENTRAL AFRIC. REPUB	0	1	0	0	0.00
CHAD	0	1	0	0	0.00
CHILE	9	62	0	1	12.68
CHINA MAINLAND	67	297	1	0	18.41
COLUMBIA	5	25	0	0	16.67
CONGO	0	1	0	0	0.00
COSTA RICA	1	28	0	0	3.45
CUBA	82	1257	1	0	6.12
CYPRUS	0	4	0	0	0.00
CZECHOSLAVKIA	77	110	1	1	41.18
CAPE VERDE	0	0	0	0	-
DJIBOUTI	0	1	0	0	0.00
DOMINICA	0	0	0	0	-
DOMINICAN REPUBLIC	1	3	0	0	25.00
ECUADOR	1	4	0	0	20.00
EGYPT	2	685	0	0	0.29
EL SALVADOR	473	18258	0	0	2.53
ETHIOPIA	559	1572	1	0	26.23
FIJI	0	1	0	0	0.00
FINLAND	0	0	0	1	-
FRANCE	1	10	0	1	9.09
GAMBIA	0	3	0	0	0.00
GERMANY, DEM. REP.	14	20	1	1	41.18
GERMANY, FED. REP.	0	9	0	1	0.00
GHANA	28	80	0	0	25.93
GREECE	0	10	0	1	0.00
GRENEDA	0	20	0	0	0.00
GUATEMALA	9	1252	0	0	0.71
GUINEA	1	4	0	0	20.00
GUYANA	4	13	0	0	23.53
HAITI	28	1117	0	0	2.45
HONDURAS	6	206	0	0	2.83

Table 1 (cont')
Asylum Admissions INS (1983 - 1985)

STATE	Appeal Approved	Appeal Denied	State of Origin	Europe	% Win
HUNGARY	115	268	1	1	30.03
INDIA	1	241	0	0	0.41
ICELAND	0	1	0	1	0.00
INDONESIA	2	16	0	0	11.11
IRAN	9556	7864	1	0	54.86
IRAQ	83	619	0	0	11.82
IRELAND	3	18	0	1	14.29
ISRAEL	1	63	0	1	1.56
ITALY	0	4	0	1	0.00
IVORY COAST	0	3	0	0	0.00
JAMAICA	0	3	0	0	0.00
JAPAN	1	2	0	0	33.33
JORDAN	2	119	0	0	1.65
KAMPUCHEA	4	6	1	0	40.00
KENYA	0	10	0	0	0.00
KOREA	5	13	1	0	27.78
KUWAIT	0	11	0	0	0.00
LAOS	5	25	1	0	16.67
LATVIA	0	1	1	1	0.00
LEBANON	20	1107	0	0	1.77
LIBERIA	15	200	0	0	6.98
LIBYA	70	55	1	0	56.00
LITHUANIA	1	1	1	1	50.00
MALAWI	1	1	0	0	50.00
MALAYSIA	0	3	0	0	0.00
MADAGASCAR	0	2	0	0	0.00
MALI	0	2	0	0	0.00
MEXICO	1	30	0	0	3.23
MOROCCO	0	12	0	0	0.00
MOZAMBIQUE	1	50	0	0	1.96
NAMIBIA	3	6	1	0	33.33
NETHERLANDS	0	0	0	1	-

Table 1 (cont')
Asylum Admissions INS (1983 - 1985)

STATE	Appeal Approved	Appeal Denied	State of Origin	Europe	% Win
NEW ZEALAND	0	2	0	1	0.00
NEPAL	0	1	0	0	0.00
NICARAGUA	1520	12983	1	0	10.48
NIGER	0	1	0	0	0.00
NIGERIA	0	23	0	0	0.00
PAKISTAN	24	337	1	0	6.65
PANAMA	0	13	0	0	0.00
PARAGUAY	0	2	0	0	0.00
PERU	1	19	0	0	5.00
PHILIPPINES	68	216	0	0	23.94
POLAND	1433	3119	1	1	31.48
PORTUGAL	0	4	0	0	0.00
ROMANIA	297	364	1	1	44.93
RWANDA	0	3	0	0	0.00
ST. LUCIA	0	1	0	0	0.00
SAUDI ARABIA	0	0	0	0	-
SENEGAL	0	1	0	0	0.00
SEYCHELLES	8	4	0	0	66.67
SIERRA LEONE	2	5	0	0	28.57
SINGAPORE	1	0	0	0	100.00
SOMALIA	56	353	0	0	13.69
SOUTH AFRICA	12	29	0	0	29.27
SPAIN	0	13	0	1	0.00
SRI LANKA	0	90	0	0	0.00
SUDAN	0	17	0	0	0.00
SURINAME	0	29	0	0	0.00
SWAZILAND	0	3	0	0	0.00
SWEDEN	0	0	0	1	-
SWITZERLAND	0	0	0	1	-
SYRIA	64	225	1	0	22.15
TAIWAN	2	9	0	0	18.18
TANZANIA	0	14	0	0	0.00
THAILAND	3	15	0	0	16.67

Table 1 (cont')
Asylum Admissions INS (1983 - 1985)

STATE	Appeal Approved	Appeal Denied	State of Origin	Europe	% Win
TOGO	0	2	0	0	0.00
TRINIDAD & TOBAGO	0	0	0	0	-
TUNISIA	0	1	0	0	0.00
TURKEY	4	60	0	1	6.25
U.S.S.R.	89	78	1	1	53.29
UGANDA	69	176	0	0	28.16
UNITED ARAB E'S	0	2	0	0	0.00
U.K, NOT H.K.	0	7	0	1	0.00
U.K., HONG KONG	0	1	0	0	0.00
UPPER VOLTA	0	0	0	0	-
URAGUAY	2	7	0	0	22.22
VENEZUELA	0	14	0	0	0.00
VIETNAM	42	133	1	0	24.00
YEMEN ADEN	1	2	1	0	33.33
YEMEN SANAA	6	5	1	0	54.55
YUGOSLAVIA	27	201	1	1	11.84
ZAIRE	7	20	0	0	25.93
ZAMBIA	0	1	0	0	0.00
ZIMBABWE	1	13	0	0	7.14

Number of Countries Listed: 137
Number of Asylum Applications: 70815
Hostile Country Applications: 43874
European Country Applications: 6317

Table 2
Refugee Admissions State Department (1982 - 1985)

KEY: State Of Origin 1 For Hostile, 0 For Non-Hostile
         Europe 1 For European State, 0 For Non-European

Mean Approvals: 42.8%

STATE	Appeal Approved	Appeal Denied	State of Origin	Europe	% Win
AFGHANISTAN	10823	2611	1	0	80.56
ALBANIA	179	517	1	0	25.72
ALGERIA	0	0	0	0	-
ANGOLA	265	152	1	0	63.55
ARGENTINA	0	1	0	0	0
BANGLADESH	0	4	0	0	0
BULGARIA	552	227	1	1	70.86
BURMA	0	23	0	0	0
CAMBODIA	11380	10181	1	0	52.78
CAMEROON	0	1	0	0	0
CHILE	0	11	0	0	0
CHINA MAINLAND	87	2244	1	0	3.73
COLUMBIA	0	3	0	0	0
CUBA	3212	2431	1	0	56.92
CZECHOSLAVKIA	3951	1664	1	1	70.37
EGYPT	4	5	0	0	44.44
EL SALVADOR	96	32	0	0	75
GERMANY, DEM. REP.	0	2	1	1	0
GHANA	0	7	0	0	0
GUINEA	0	1	0	0	0
HAITI	0	0	0	0	-
HONDURAS	0	1	0	0	0
HUNGARY	2148	1457	1	1	59.58
INDIA	7	1	0	0	87.5
INDONESIA	0	48	0	0	0
IRAN	7412	2595	1	0	74.07
IRAQ	4029	707	0	0	85.07
ISRAEL	0	73	0	0	0

Table 2 (cont')
Refugee Admissions State Department (1982 - 1985)

STATE	Appeal Approved	Appeal Denied	State of Origin	Europe	% Win
JORDAN	0	0	0	0	-
KAMPUCHEA	50089	16913	1	0	74.76
LAOS	21737	2994	1	0	87.89
LEBANON	0	7	0	0	0
LIBERIA	0	1	0	0	0
LESOTHO	22	5	0	0	81.48
LIBYA	0	15	1	0	0
MACAU	11	4	0	0	73.33
MALAWI	30	11	0	0	73.17
MALAYSIA	0	5	0	0	0
MAURITIUS	0	1	0	0	0
MEXICO	0	2	0	0	0
MOROCCO	0	0	0	0	-
MOZAMBIQUE	53	7	0	0	88.33
NAMIBIA	51	38	1	0	57.3
NEW CALEDONIA	0	1	0	0	0
NICARAGUA	6	72	1	0	7.69
NIGERIA	0	0	0	0	-
PAKISTAN	9	7	1	0	56.25
PHILIPPINES	92	40	0	0	69.7
POLAND	19708	7361	1	1	72.81
ROMANIA	15924	2033	1	1	88.68
SAO TOME & PRINCIPE	1	0	0	0	100
SENEGAL	0	0	0	0	-
SINGAPORE	0	5	0	0	0
SOMALIA	0	8	0	0	0
SOUTH AFRICA	68	75	0	0	47.55
SRI LANKA	0	5	0	0	0
SUDAN	17	1	0	0	94.44
SYRIA	53	13	1	0	80.3
TAIWAN	12	3	0	0	80
TANZANIA	0	0	0	0	-
THAILAND	0	5	0	0	0

Table 2 (cont')
Refugee Admissions State Department (1982 - 1985)

KEY: State Of Origin   1 For Hostile, 0 For Non-Hostile
          Europe   1 For European State, 0 For Non-European

STATE	Appeal Approved	Appeal Denied	State of Origin	Europe	% Win
TURKEY	1	1	1	1	50
U.S.S.R.	5587	237	1	1	95.93
UGANDA	10	1	0	0	90.91
U.K., HONG KONG	517	268	0	0	65.86
VIETNAM	103357	11757	1	0	89.79
YEMEN ADEN	0	2	1	0	0
YUGOSLAVIA	26	227	1	0	10.28
ZAIRE	86	24	0	0	78.18
ZIMBABWE	5	0	0	0	100

Number of Countries: 71
Number of Refugee Applications: 342, 388
Hostile Country Applications: 335, 930
European Country Applications: 82, 667

Appendix F

Sources Of Support For Legal Services Organizations

The sources of support for legal services organizations are listed in order of importance, where the percenrage listed next to the source of organizational support is the percentage of organizations which indicate that they rely on a particular source.

SOURCE OF SUPPORT	% Of Orgs. Listing As Source Of Funds
Private Foundations	51
State Government	33
Religious Organizations	30
Federal Government	29
Bar Organizations	16
Individual Donors	15
Law Schools/Alumni	13
Local Government	7
Sale of Publications	4
Law Firm Donations	4
Nominal Fees	2
Other Public Interest Organizations	2
Corporations	0

n = 56

5

A Synthesis and a General Model

Developing a general theory of public law is an ambitious task for anyone to undertake, particularly at the early stages of one's career. Yet perhaps it is best done early because one retains a sufficient amount of bravado and has not yet been subject to a sufficient amount of criticism from one's professional peers. Nevertheless, I have had some fortunate results from early public law analyses of court cases, all of which were directed in some way at discovering the conditions under which political and environmental variables appear to affect judicial decision making.

In some instances, there was temporary disappointment as my initial hypotheses were completely unsupported by the statistical analysis of objective data. So it was, for example, when I discovered that in rape sentencing cases, (Case Study 2, Chapter 2) political variables appear not to have affected court outcomes. This led, however, to discovery as I pondered the question of why political variables are important in some cases and not in others. Another surprise that ultimately generated my "judicial constituency" variable occurred in the analysis of federal court outcomes in asylum-related appeals (Cast Study 1, Chapter 2), where region was not significantly related to outcome. I began to wonder about the characteristics of individuals within judicial circuits and districts, and whether there might be a certain target group, such as immigrants, that were particularly affected by judicial decisions in asylum-related appeals and in other court cases.

Hence, through a combination of accident and rational planning, I generated what I believe to be interesting research findings that, though preliminary, shed some light on situations in which political and environmental variables are related to judicial outcomes. These findings were consolidated into a general model of public law, which will be more easily accepted if one sees it in its proper light, as a heuristic device intended not to be a comprehensive final word, but as a model that stimulates thought and future research. With this apologia, I now proceed to my general model of public law.

Political factors are likely to count in federal district court decision making when the case involves a major, publicized issue, along the lines suggested by Page et al. (1984) and other theorists (Miller and Stokes 1963) in their discussions of congressional decision making. Specifically, "apolitical" federal court judges are likely to take into account such political factors as the preferences of judicial constituents, their own partisan affiliation (or the affiliation of their appointing president), and interest group involvement when the cases involve issues that are regularly reported by the media, receive public scrutiny, and tend to conform with divisions between the Republican and Democratic parties. For example, in Case Study 1 (Chapter 2), on federal court decision making in cases involving political refugees and asylees, it was observed that federal judges decided these politically divisive cases in a politicized manner: the judges were seemingly influenced by their partisan affiliations (Democrats ruled in favor of refugees), interest groups (interest group participation bolstered a refugee's chances of prevailing in litigation), and constituency preferences (judges responded positively when there were large immigrant populations in their areas).

Similarly, in Case Study 4 (Chapter 3), when federal district courts adjudicated cases involving the major, publicized issue of abortion, judicial outcomes were related to political pressures, including the involvement of pro-abortion interest groups in litigation.

In contrast, when the issue involved was not a major, publicized issue, judges were less likely to take political factors into account when making their decisions. For example, in sentencing individuals convicted of rape, state court judges in Montana (Case Study 2, Chapter 2) seemed to ignore their judicial constituents in their decisions (defined as politically powerful women in their areas) and the partisanship of their constituents.

Where the litigation issue is minor and non-publicized, judges are relatively free of normal political pressures related to partisanship, constituency preferences, and interest group involvement in litigation. In these cases, they may be influenced by factors more relevant to the case at hand. In the rape sentencing decisions discussed, for example, judges took into account legally relevant factors such as the crime rate and whether multiple charges were pending against a defendant.

Similarly, in the context of administrative adjudication, other factors that are more relevant to the politics of administrative tribunals appear to influence decision makers. For example, in the comparison of administrative versus judicial decision making in asylum-related appeals (Case Study 5, Chapter 4), it was discovered that the BIA, unlike the federal courts, was not influenced by the involvement of interest groups in asylum-related appeals. Instead, it tended to conform with the administrative bias of the immigration bureaucracy in favor of aliens from hostile countries of origin.

Even among litigation issues that are minor and not regularly publicized, such as international extradition, a second category of cases in which political factors are likely to count are ones that somehow affect politically powerful groups within the United States. For example, in an analysis of federal court outcomes in international extradition cases (Case Study 3, Chapter 2) federal court judges did not respond to the usual political factors of interest group involvement, partisan affiliation, and the preferences of judicial constituents. Instead, decisions in these cases seemed to be related to "ethnic politics": Litigants were more likely to defeat a request for international extradition when they were linked to the Irish Republican Army, as, for example, when their crime was committed on the behalf of the IRA, and to the organized and powerful Irish community in the United States. In contrast, litigants who were unsupported by any ethnic community in the United States, or who were linked to a weak and politically powerless ethnic group (as in the case of Palestinian litigants who committed their crimes on the behalf of the Palestine Liberation Organization), were more likely to lose their cases and be extradited.

In Case Study 4 (Chapter 3), federal court outcomes in abortion cases were linked to the involvement of pro-abortion interest groups, while other political factors were not significantly related to outcome. These unrelated factors included the partisanship of judges or their appointing presidents, the preferences of judicial constituents (politically powerful congresswomen within judges' states), and the involvement of anti-abortion groups in litigation.

Hence, a general theory of public law might postulate that courts, whether their members are appointed or elected, are expected to respond to their political environment when (1) the case affects the interests of powerful interest groups in the United States; and/or (2) the issue involved in the case is a major, publicized one.

When the second condition is met, some or all of the following political factors may affect judicial decision making: the preferences of judicial constituents; the partisanship of the judges involved or that of their appointing presidents; and the involvement of interest groups in the case.

Geographic region becomes significant when the issue is one with high ideological content (Yarnold 1990a, 1990b, 1991). Race relations cases have historically divided the federal judiciary along regional lines (Richardson and Vines 1978); so also do environmental cases (Wenner 1982; Wenner and Dutter 1988). It was earlier hypothesized that region would be significantly related to outcome in abortion cases due to the highly ideological nature of the abortion issue. In accordance with these predictions, in federal court cases involving abortion (Case Study 4, Chapter 3), federal court outcomes exhibited regional variance.

In light of these findings and the enormous research efforts of preceding public law researchers, the traditional concept of the judiciary as a neutral interpreter of the law in specific factual cases has been relegated to the status of an outdated judicial axiom. One is not even certain that it is a desirable normative objective. Given the extent to which federal courts are influenced by their political environment and enthusiastically embrace their policy-making function, it is not unreasonable to suggest, as in Case Study 1 (Chapter 2), that this unelected policy maker ought to be subject to some form of popular control, such as elections.

III

New Approaches: Combining Public Law with Pluralism and Theories about Social Movements

6

Social Movements and Public Interest Litigation Groups

CASE STUDY 6: THE RISE OF SOCIAL MOVEMENTS AND PUBLIC INTEREST GROUPS

The Origins of Social Movements: A People's Choice of Natural Law over Positive Law When the Two Conflict

Throughout history, there has been tension between our adherence to either positive law or natural law. A not uncommon reason for conflict among men and nations has been that one participant in the conflict enacted a written norm or customary practice, or relied on conventional law in undertaking certain actions, with unjust results. In spite of the argument that the actor's activities conformed with "conventional" or "positive" law, consisting of prevailing laws, norms, or practices, these activities seemed to violate a higher moral law, or our innate "natural law" precepts, which originate either from our ability to reason or from revelations from God.

Early philosophers were aware of the dichotomy between natural law and positive law. Aristotle, in his *Nichomachean Ethics*, makes a distinction between justice that is natural and justice that is conventional. Conventional justice consists of written norms that are established by the members of a political society largely due to necessity. Natural justice, however, consists of rules that are common among all people according to nature and are perceived though unwritten, as each person carries within him a conception of justice (Edwards 1981).

Plato further articulated the notion of natural law as immutable and derived from the order of nature. Natural law precepts are aimed at attaining ultimate goodness. We may find harmony and justice only if we live in conformity with the truths of nature (Edwards 1981). In *The Commonwealth*, Cicero followed the lead of the Greek philosophers in postulating the existence of a body of natural law:

> There is in fact a true law—namely right reason—which is in accordance with nature, applies to all men, and is unchangeable and eternal. . . . Neither the Senate nor the people can absolve us from our obligation to obey this law, and it requires no Sextus Aelius to expound it and interpret it. . . . [B]inding at all times and upon all people; and there will be, as it were, one common master and ruler of men, namely God, who is the author of this law. . . . The man who will not obey it will abandon his better self, and, in denying the true nature of a man, will thereby suffer the severest of penalties, though he has escaped all the other consequences which men call punishment. (Edwards 1981: 29)

There were two schools of thought among early philosophers regarding the origins of natural law. "In the Aristotelian sense, law is the 'right reason' " (Edwards 1981: 33). It was believed that through use of our reason, we may become aware of our natural inclinations. Since these natural inclinations are derived from nature, and therefore good, whatever we do in conformity with these inclinations is also good. In contrast, anything that hampers a natural inclination is evil.

On the other side of the natural law debate were early Christian philosophers who believed that natural law is only divined through our relationship to God. Yet despite an "imperfect" relationship with God, St. Paul said, we may still be capable of perceiving some of the dictates of natural law:

> For when the Gentiles, which have not the law, do by nature the things contained in the law, these having not the law, are a law unto themselves, which shew the work of laws written in their hearts, their conscience also bearing witness and their thoughts the meanwhile accusing or else excusing one another. (Edwards 1981: 35)

The contrasting views of natural law as derived from reason or from divine revelation were finally reconciled by St. Thomas Aquinas, who postulated that our knowledge of natural law is derived from two sources: (1) from nature, in which we are capable of rational discernment of truth; and (2) from supernature, in which we derive truth through divine revelation (Edwards 1981).

The fact that early Greek, Roman, and Christian philosophers recognized the existence of natural law precepts, as distinct from conventional or positive law precepts, lends strong support to the argument that tension has existed between our adherence either to natural or to positive law. These writings further suggest that we have a choice between the two and that it is our responsibility to follow natural law precepts when these conflict with conventional written and unwritten rules, norms, and practices.

To a great extent, social movements in the United States may be explained as a collective decision by persons and organizations to follow natural law over positive law when the two conflict.

Social movements have been defined as follows:

[A] social movement is characterized by activity directed toward changing institutions and behaviors of importance to a society, as opposed to peripheral institutions or routine behaviors. Another defining feature of a social movement is its mode of political expression, often consisting of unconventional tactics and behavior, such as civil disobedience, organizing demonstrations, breaking up into small groups for the purpose of "consciousness raising," and even the threat or actual use of violence. (McFarland 1983: 338)

Social movements call for fundamental change in the positive law when the positive law does not coincide with natural law precepts. Members of social movements are willing to engage in unconventional tactics to achieve their goals, even if this means that they must violate positive law. McFarland points to a number of social movements in the United States during the last three decades: the civil rights movement, the women's movement, the governmental reform movement, the consumer protection movement, the environmental protection movement, the peace movement, the fundamentalist Christian movement, the tax revolt movement of 1977–80, and the gay rights movement. Since McFarland wrote, one new movement, the sanctuary movement, may be added to the list. These movements have all been characterized by a disaffection on the part of movement participants with the positive law and a willingness to engage in non-traditional activity that often contravenes positive law precepts.

For example, the civil rights movement of the 1950s and early 1960s had a core objective of causing fundamental change in the positive law of the United States, which allowed for both public and private discrimination on the basis of race (McFarland 1983). Throughout the United States, blacks and whites were segregated; they did not, for example, attend the same public or private schools or use the same public or private accommodations. The law either enforced segregation of the races (for example, with respect to public schools) or tacitly failed to interfere with segregation (for example, with respect to restrictive covenants in leases and other documents). Various individuals and groups reacted to what appeared to be an immoral and repugnant positive law that conflicted with natural law precepts of justice and equality; their combined actions culminated in what has come to be known as the civil rights movement.

The activities and strategies of participants in the civil rights movement ranged widely, from the legalistic approach of groups like the National Association for the Advancement of Colored People (NAACP) which fought a laborious battle in state and federal courts to abolish discriminatory laws, to the civil disobedience of followers of the Reverend Martin Luther King Jr., to the confrontational, illegal, and often violent strategies employed by groups like the Black Muslims and the Black Panthers (McFarland 1983).

In much the same way, the sanctuary movement that arose in the United States in the early 1980s was a response to what appeared to be an immoral and repugnant positive law that failed to provide refuge to persons from Central American countries. The United States' positive law conflicted with natural law precepts of charity and granting sanctuary to those displaced by natural and man-made disasters. Individuals and organizations responded to this dilemma by making a collective choice in favor of natural law precepts and in favor of providing these aliens with refuge in the United States. The sanctuary movement is, at its core, an illegal attempt to bypass the legal structures of U.S. immigration laws and procedures. Participants in the sanctuary movement have varied strategies; some overtly violate the law, while others offer assistance to more active participants in the movement and the movement's beneficiaries but remain within the parameters of the positive law.

The impetus to a social movement is collective disaffection with positive law. The sanctuary movement originated in the frustration of many individuals and organizations with the failure of U.S. immigration laws to provide refuge to Central Americans feeling from deteriorating conditions in El Salvador and Guatemala. Both of these countries were torn by civil war, and those who sought shelter in the United States often came with reports of serious human rights abuses, including torture. Refugees from Central America are able, pursuant to the United States' immigration laws, to apply for either political asylum or withholding of deportation on the basis that they have a well-founded fear of persecution or that there is a clear probability that they will be persecuted in their countries of origin. However, many critics note that the immigration bureaucracy favors in refugees and asylum admissions those fleeing from hostile countries, defined as countries with communist, socialist, or leftist forms of government (Preston 1986; Helton 1984; Loescher and Scanlan 1986; Yarnold 1990b, 1990c, 1991b). Because El Salvador and Guatemala maintain good relations with the United States, aliens from these countries are not likely to be successful applicants for asylum and withholding. Hence, Central American refugees are clearly "refugees without refuge" (Yarnold 1990b, 1990c, 1991b).

The fact that U.S. immigration law provides no remedy for the vast majority of refugees from Central America has been attested to by many commentators. Among these are individuals within the sanctuary movement, who initially attempted to help Central American refugees through legal immigration channels. These individuals and organizations repeatedly document violations of these aliens' limited due process rights by the immigration bureaucracy in the course of their legal attempts to obtain refuge in the United States. There are also reports that the aliens are often not informed of their right to apply for political asylum and withholding of deportation, or of other statutory and constitutional rights. Susan Gzesch, an immigration attorney who inspected detention camps in Texas, suggests:

The vast majority of Salvadorans are voluntarily returned to their own country by the INS without ever having had the opportunity to apply for political asylum. Many of them return never knowing such an opportunity exists, or if they did know, they were discouraged from applying by INS authorities, who see their primary work as returning undocumented entrants quickly. (Golden and McConnell 1986: 41)

Golden and McConnell state that lawyers working through immigration channels on behalf of Central American refugees had "documented violations of due process so consistent as to constitute a policy" (Golden and McConnell 1986: 41).

Due process and other violations on the part of the immigration bureaucracy with respect to asylum and withholding applicants from El Salvador and Guatemala would not be as significant if these aliens were obtaining substantive relief. This is not, however, the case. Most aliens from these countries who apply for either type of relief are unsuccessful. Goldman and McConnell (1986: 42) comment:

Even if allowed to apply for political asylum, however, Central Americans rarely are granted asylum. . . . More statistics show that nationwide over twenty-two thousand applied during 1982; only seventy-four were granted asylum. For the year 1984, out of thirteen thousand Salvadoran asylum requests, only 325 were granted.

These commentators also suggest that a lack of publicly available information about background conditions in El Salvador and Guatemala keeps most people in the United States uninformed about the conditions in which Central American refugees, deported to their countries of origin, are forced to live. Hence, public opinion in the United States has not yet risen to the level of opposing current practices of the immigration bureaucracy with respect to its treatments of these refugees, and public pressure is not likely to force policy changes in this area. Further, both private citizens and policy makers in the United States are, according to these authors, intentionally misinformed about conditions in El Salvador, Guatemala, and Honduras, since most government reports indicate that human rights abuses in these countries are diminishing and that these countries are engaged in democratization when many suggest conditions have either remained the same or have deteriorated.

In response to an inability to obtain natural law through the mechanism of the positive law, persons and organizations in the United States who became involved in the sanctuary movement increasingly abandoned resort to positive law. Some went beyond this, however, and actively violated the law in order to provide refuge to Central American refugees. One such individual, who can be called one of the founders of the U.S. sanctuary movement, is Jim Corbett, who was the first in the United States to bring a Central American refugee across the border to safety. This act took place in the spring of 1981, when Corbett transported a Salvadoran from the Mexican border to John Fife's Presbyterian church in Tucson, Arizona. John Fife explained how he came to illegally harbor aliens in his church:

> Initially we were involved with undocumented people, raising bond money, and getting lawyers to assist people who had already been arrested by the INS. We had been doing this for six months or so. Well, I am not mentally retarded and after that much involvement with legal defense efforts, I realized that they were neither effective nor moral. After a while it became apparent that this was an exercise in futility. You recognize very quickly that nobody is going to get asylum except a tiny minority. (*Catholic Agitator* 1984)

Jim Corbett was one of the first in the sanctuary movement to encourage others to abandon reliance on the positive law in this area for adherence only to moral precepts, or natural law. In an article submitted to the National Lawyers Guild's Central American Refugee Defense Fund Newsletter, dated June 6, 1986, Corbett wrote:

> The defense of human rights by the church is faith-based and worship initiated, but we need look neither to heaven, nor to the Bible nor to corporate conscience for the higher law that overrules unjust laws. . . . The community that dedicates itself to doing justice exposes and challenges an outlaw administration in ways that simple resistance to injustice does not, because compliance with human rights law that is being violated by the state requires that a community assume on-going administrative functions that breach the regulatory "territory" assigned to government officials. . . . [C]oncerning the screening, placement, and protection of Central American refugees, for example, the sanctuary network is an emergency alternative to the INS. (National Lawyers' Guild, June 6, 1986: 3)

At another time, Corbett explained resort to illegality:

> When the government itself sponsors the torture of entire peoples and then makes it a felony to shelter those seeking refuge, law-abiding protest merely trains us to live with atrocity. . . . The presence of undocumented refugees here among us makes the definitive nature of our choice particularly clear and concrete. Where oppression rules, the way of peace is necessarily insurgent. (Golden and McConnell 1986: 37)

In fact, the route chosen by Corbett seemed to be more effective than a purely legal one. By 1984, Corbett had brought 700 Central American refugees into the

United States. At the same time, few Central American refugees who pursued legal channels obtained asylum or withholding.

Ted Loder, senior minister of the First United Methodist Church of Germantown, a church in Philadelphia that provided sanctuary for a Guatemalan refugee family, also writes of the choice he faced when confronted with an immoral positive law:

> Still, to be human at all, you—I—have to make moral choices and take moral actions. The evidence, incomplete as it may be, is persuasive that some things are simply wrong. Injustice, exploitation, oppression, tyranny are arguably real in our common life, even if the solutions are arguable. The whisper—or scream—of conscience can be ignored only at peril to one's humanity. (Loder 1986: 38–39)

The comments of those involved in the sanctuary movement in the United States suggest that their choice to resort to illegal acts, which contravene positive law, was compelled by their greater loyalty to moral or natural law precepts. As suggested earlier, social movements generally originate from conflict between principles of positive and natural law.

One Link between Organized Interest Groups and Social Movements: Communication of Ideas of a Social Movement by Interest Groups

One of the most significant links between social movements and organized interest groups is that organized interests may act as a communications network for social movements, facilitating the communication of their major ideas in a way that may legitimize movements, bring public pressure for policy change, attract entrepreneurial politicians who adopt all or part of the social movements' platform, and effect policy change (McFarland 1983; Freeman 1975). Thus, social movements are dependent on organized interests; the failure of organized interests to communicate any of the ideas of a social movement may result in the failure of the social movement to cause any significant policy change.

One question that arises relates to which interest groups are likely to act as the essential link between the ideas of a social movement and a political system. It is suggested that there are various types of interest groups that form and maintain concentric circles around a political system. Interest groups that are the most dependent on the political system and whose structure and activities are largely shaped by the political system are not likely to be the first to embrace the ideas of a social movement, particularly when the participants in a social movement resort to illegal conduct. This first layer of organizations will be referred to as "entrenched organizations." This term emphasizes that these organizations have become, in a significant way, a part of the political system. Entrenched organizations adhere primarily to positive law precepts, even when these conflict with moral or natural law precepts. Like government agencies, the main objective of these organizations has become, in spite of previous orientations, organizational maintenance. Because identification with the non-mainstream policies of a social movement and with the illegal activities of participants in a social movement may jeopardize their reputation and the financial resources available, entrenched organizations are not likely to be the first to adopt the ideas of a social movement. Such organizations may only become involved in promoting the ideas of a social movement after these ideas have been legitimized and publicized by other interest groups and politicians.

Entrenched organizations are of two types: social welfare organizations and legal organizations. For reasons that will be discussed at a later point, legal interest groups may be far less amenable to the ideas of a social movement than are social welfare interest groups.

Although groups fall between the categories, for the sake of simplicity, the second layer of interest groups will be referred to as "fringe organizations." Fringe organizations provide the important communication system for the ideas of a social movement. They tend to be less dependent on the political system for support, structure, and shaping the strategies employed by the organizations. Unlike entrenched organizations, which are primarily oriented toward organizational maintenance, fringe organizations are primarily policy-oriented, pursuing policy goals even when this pursuit interferes with organizational maintenance. Fringe organizations tend to follow moral or natural law precepts when these conflict with positive law precepts. Fringe organizations do not have the same stake in the political system as do entrenched organizations. Hence, fringe organizations may adopt the ideas of a social movement more readily than will entrenched organizations, even when a social movement's ideas and conduct are unconventional, because they do not have to protect established reputations for the sake of maintaining financial support.

Fringe Organizations. Fringe organizations are motivated by natural law concepts and often promote these concepts in a manner that conflicts with or directly violates the positive law. Fringe organizations are more responsive to the natural law precepts advanced by a social movement than are entrenched organizations, which are based in positive law. Fringe organizations do not strive for organizational maintenance to the same extent as do entrenched organizations, and for this reason, their continued existence tends to be constantly in question. Due to their adoption of unpopular policy positions or modes of conduct, these organizations may have difficulty attracting and maintaining financial support from government, business, private foundations, other organizations, and other sources that are established and have a stake in the larger political system. Hence, fringe organizations may be of limited duration and may encounter official and unofficial resistance, which limits their ability to pursue their policy goals.

The most significant point to note with respect to fringe organizations is that they are often the first or only "voice" of a social movement. Hence, these organizations provide social movements with a communications system that alerts other organizations, policy makers, and the general public to the core ideas of the social movement (Freeman 1975). The following discussion examines fringe organizations, both secular and non-secular.

Religious fringe organizations. History is replete with examples of religious organizations that have come into conflict with positive law due to their adherence to their perception of a higher, moral law. In the United States, various religious organizations actively engage in efforts to either change the existing positive law or interfere with its administration. For example, particularly in the late 1980s and early 1990s, anti-abortion church groups engaged in systematic lobbying efforts to replace laws that allowed women to obtain abortions with laws that prohibit them. Some of these religious organizations, however, went beyond legal mechanisms when legal methods failed. Members of religious organizations engaged in sit-ins at abortion clinics, obstructive picketing, and even bombing of clinics. Their justification for these "extra-legal" and "non-legal" methods was that they were seeking to promote a natural law precept—protection of the unborn—that takes precedence over conflicting positive law precepts.

To the extent that religious organizations adhere to natural law precepts over the positive law, they share much in common with participants in social movements. Religious organizations have been rather hospitable to social movements, adopting the major policy positions of movements and serving to communicate these ideas to the general public, other organizations, and policy makers. Since the 1950s, for example, religious organizations have acted as communications systems for the Civil Rights movement, the peace movement, and the fundamentalist Christian movement, among others (McFarland 1983). Due to their historic commitment to natural law, religious organizations generally play an important role in social movements, unless the core ideas of social movements conflict with the religious dogma of these organizations. The identification of religious organizations with the ideas of a social movement gives to these ideas a measure of legitimacy.

Religious organizations that have become involved in social movements are properly classified as fringe organizations. Crucial to their independence from political systems is that they rarely rely to a great extent on government subsidies for support, or on private foundations, wealthy individuals, business and professional organizations, and other interests that are entrenched or have a great stake in the existing political and economic system. Instead, religious organizations are supported primarily by their congregations. Hence, these organizations are not concerned with maintaining a reputation for seeking conventional policy goals and engaging in conventional political activity in order to ensure their continued financial support by government or persons and organizations entrenched in the existing political and economic system. This is not to suggest that these religious organizations are impervious to the political system. In the United States, for example, church organizations active in the sanctuary movement feared the loss of their tax-exempt status and also feared criminal indictments against their members. In spite of these penalties, religious organizations continue to advance natural law precepts.

A prime example of the communication link between fringe religious organizations and social movements arises in the context of the Civil Rights movement. During the early 1950s, black Protestant churches were used to communicate the ideas of the Civil Rights movement. The movement's acknowledged leader, Dr. Martin Luther King, Jr., was a Baptist minister. In these religious organizations, ministers appealed to a higher, moral law that contrasted sharply with a positive law that allowed for both de facto and de jure discrimination against blacks. The Civil Rights movement was communicated through the churches to blacks, who then engaged in protests, civil disobedience, and, in some instances, violent activity. Through these acts, the larger white population became informed of the major ideas of the Civil Rights movement. Policy changes were to occur after the adoption of some of the major precepts of the social movement by both entrenched persons and organizations (such as the American Civil Liberties Union) and political entrepreneurs, such as President Lyndon B. Johnson (McFarland 1983).

The independence of black churches, which articulated the central ideas of the Civil Rights movement, was attributable to the fact that they were not dependent on any governmental unit for financial support, or on established interests, such as other organizations, wealthy contributors, private foundations, and business. Their activity was subsidized by contributions from church members.

The sanctuary movement, which arose in the United States in the early 1980s, provides an even better example of the communication link between fringe religious organizations and the ideas of a social movement than does the civil rights movement of the 1950s because the sanctuary movement is a church-initiated trend that attracted little support from non-religious organizations. The religious base of the sanctuary movement is best illustrated by the following statement, contained in an informational pamphlet distributed by the Chicago Religious Task Force on Central America (CRTFCA), in February 1988. CR-TFCA is the national coordinating body for the sanctuary movement.

> We believe that God's revelation is principally discovered among the world's oppressed and most vulnerable. Both the Torah and the Gospel compel us to choose sides with the poor, creating a covenant of solidarity with those struggling for life and justice. God chose to act decisively for the liberation of the Hebrews from bondage in Egypt. The prophets continually advocated for the rights of the poor, sojourners, widows, and orphans. The ministry of Jesus began with the proclamation to "set free those who are oppressed." (CRTFCA 1988)

In a June 1987 edition of *Basta*, a journal produced by CRTFCA, Jon Sobrino (1987) discussed the theological justification for the sanctuary movement.

> The sanctuary movement is theologically justified because it is a way of defending the lives of the poor and thus of believing in and responding

to the God of Christian biblical faith. The central theological thesis is the following: God is the defender of the lives of the poor and makes that defense something ultimate, unconditional and higher than everything else; every human being and, therefore, all believers especially have the right and the obligation to defend the lives of the poor. (*Basta* June 1987: 19–20)

By December 1987, *Basta* reported, there were 448 sanctuary locations in the United States. Of these, 405, or slightly over 90 percent, were organized either by religious congregations (404) or by seminaries (1). Only 43, or 10 percent, were organized by non-religious entities, including cities (27) and universities (16) (*Basta* December 1987: 2).

Sanctuary has a long historical tradition in both Christian and Jewish history. During World War II, Protestant and Catholic churches throughout the world gave refuge to Jews persecuted by Germans. These historical precedents gave the sanctuary movement carried on by religious organizations additional legitimacy and urgency. Participants in the sanctuary movement chose natural law precepts over positive law precepts, and chose to violate the positive law when this appeared necessary.

For some time after the sanctuary movement was launched by Jim Corbett in 1981, it remained a local phenomenon, based out of John Fife's church in Tucson and supported by the Tucson Ecumenical Council, a coalition of 60 Tucson churches. Before adopting illegal strategies, Corbett and the Tucson Ecumenical Council attempted legal strategies for helping aliens from Guatemala, Honduras, and El Salvador. Their joint efforts raised $100,000 to bail out Central American refugees kept in a regional detention center. Ultimately, their efforts to help these aliens through legal channels failed. Of the 100 refugees they bonded out, only 5 percent were able to obtain political asylum. In order to raise the sum of $100,000, ministers and members of congregations mortgaged their homes. The Tucson group came to agree:

[T]here is no justice for Central American refugees under present INS policy and with present State Department and INS personnel. The system and the foreign policy that controls it are misconceived. For any church or agency to encourage refugees to voluntarily enter this system, other than as a last resort, would be at best a mistake, and at worst, complicity in the violation of human rights. Evasion services, sanctuary, and an extensive underground railroad were the answer. (Golden and McConnell 1986: 46)

McConnell (1986: 9) comments in a June 1986 edition of *Basta*: "The Sanctuary Movement began in 1982 in direct response to the refugees fleeing the violence and death squad killings in El Salvador and Guatemala." The first pastor in the United States to publicly declare that his church was a sanctuary was Reverend John Fife in March 1982. Shortly after, five East Bay churches in California were also declared places of sanctuary.

Soon after these proclamations, however, the resources of the early sanctuary churches were severely tapped. Leaders of the sanctuary movement increasingly sought to make the movement national in scope. In August 1982, CRTFCA, a coalition of local religious groups, accepted its first Central American refugees. Corbett approached the organization and requested that it become the national coordinator of the underground railroad. CRTFCA accepted his offer and currently occupies this leadership position in the sanctuary movement; "from coast to coast a railroad would extend as far north as Canada and as far east as Boston" (Golden and McConnell 1986: 52). The number of religious organizations that offered sanctuary to Central American refugees, according to one account, numbered only 30 in 1982 (Golden and McConnell 1986: 53). In December 1987, *Basta* reported a total of 448 sanctuary locations nationwide; over 90 percent of these are affiliated with religious organizations (*Basta* December 1987: 2). The increase in sites demonstrates that the sanctuary movement has grown from a local phenomenon to a national social movement. In fact, the sanctuary movement even transcends national boundaries. By making links with Central American and Canadian sanctuary providers, which also tend to be religious organizations, the sanctuary movement has become international in scope (*Basta* September 1986: 3)4).

Basta lists as the goals of the sanctuary movement: "to protect as many as possible of the refugees whom conscience demands we not allow our government to deport; to let our witness function as pressure against inhumane policies which both create refugees and then deny them haven" (*Basta* September 1986: 14).

By September 1986, *Basta* was reporting that the second goal, that of publicizing the plight of refugees and changing public policy in the United States, had failed: "After four years, Sanctuary and the U.S. undeclared war in Central America is not a national issue. Information and debate on Central America has not reached a mass level" (*Basta* September 1986: 13).

CRTFCA staff member Robin Semer, in a March 3, 1988, interview, indicated that the sanctuary movement had helped thousands of Central American refugees. She conceded that this was a minute fraction of Central American refugees in need of assistance, but suggested that Central American refugees who came to the United States and found sanctuary alerted U.S. religious congregations and the public to the intolerable conditions in Central American countries.

Nevertheless, a contributor to *Basta*, Archbishop Rivera y Damas (1986), reaffirmed his commitment to the sanctuary movement in December 1986, in spite of its partial failure: "Sanctuary will continue as long as the war in Central America continues to bomb civilians, abuse the rights of citizens and create refugees and displaced persons. Only when the war ends and El Salvador and Guatemala are sanctuaries for their people will the Sanctuary Movement stop" (*Basta* December 1986: 25).

Individuals and religious organizations engaged in smuggling aliens from Central America into the United States, transporting, and harboring them were violating federal statutes that prohibit these actions. In February 1984, the first arrests of members of the sanctuary movement Stacey Merkdt and Dianne Muhlenkamp were made. In April 1984, Jack Elder was also arrested; all three were affiliated with Casa Romero, a Central American refugee assistance center sponsored by the Catholic church near the Rio Grande. After her arrest, Stacey Merkdt wrote: "How long can we close our eyes to the 'disappeareds,' to the continued increase in killing, to the torture and to the Salvadoran government's participation in this? Who is the criminal? Who will allow it to continue?" (Golden and McConnell 1986: 68).

A contributor to *Basta* made the following summary of the "Tucson trial":

The government's short-term tactic, criminal conviction, was temporarily successful in pure result-oriented terms. Eight of eleven people were convicted on 18 of 71 original charges. . . . However, the convictions were extracted at great cost. Sanctuary supporters, along with most defendants, experienced their first taste of the U.S. justice system: its operation was not fair. (*Basta* September 1986: 23)

The conclusion of this contributor to *Basta* is:

The fundamental lesson, as always, is that only organized movements cause change. The legal system is another branch of the political system that we must use toward the end of justice at every turn. But as our history teaches us, the legal system often lags behind morality and justice. (*Basta* September 1986: 25)

These statements are typical of individuals and religious organizations who participate in the sanctuary movement. There is a willingness to violate the positive law when this is necessary to meet the demands of natural law. The religious organizations that became involved in the sanctuary movement are properly described as fringe organizations because they were loyal to natural law rather than positive law precepts. They also did not have a reputation to uphold for the purpose of securing contributions from the government or other entrenched interests that had flourished in the existing political and economic system and thus had a stake in the maintenance of the status quo. The independence of religious organizations may be attributed to the fact that they received most of their support from their congregations. The independence of fringe religious organizations, however, is not without cost. They have often met with official and unofficial repression. Supporters of sanctuary claim that sanctuary workers have had to contend with criminal indictments, break-ins at churches, suspected telephone taps, and arrests of refugees (*Basta* September 1986: 23).

Religious organizations involved in the sanctuary movement are policy-oriented and unlike entrenched organizations, have not directed much attention to organizational maintenance. Because they initiated and attempt to carry out the agenda of the sanctuary movement, they served as an important communications system, bringing the core ideas of the movement to other organizations, to the general public, and to public policy makers.

One of the most important mechanisms through which the ideas of any social movement, including the sanctuary movement, are communicated to other sectors of society is the media. Members of religious fringe organizations that support the sanctuary movement and are active participants in it have made use of the media as a communications tool, contacting members of the press whenever an affiliate organization offered sanctuary to refugees from Central America and inviting press coverage of the trials of participants in the movement.

Although these efforts have not yet had a significant impact on U.S. policy with respect to the governments of El Salvador and Guatemala or their refugees, the fact that the number of religious and secular organizations that provide sanctuary to Central American refugees, an illegal act, has increased from 30 in 1982 to 448 in December 1987 indicates that the core ideas of the sanctuary movement have been adopted by some segments of U.S. society. Most importantly, the concept of sanctuary has gained the support of religious leaders from the largest religious organizations in the United States (including Baptist, Brethren, Disciples of Christ, Episcopalian, Jewish, New Jewish Agenda, Lutheran, Mennonite, Methodist, Presbyterian, Quaker, Roman Catholic, United Church of Christ, Unitarian Universalist, other Protestant, and Ecumenical). These religious leaders have a communications system through which they may spread the ideas of the sanctuary movement to their congregation and, hence, the general public (McFarland 1983). If the public comes to support a more even-handed application of the laws relating to refugees and asylees from these countries, "political entrepreneurs" may attempt to garner electoral support by adopting the policy platform of the sanctuary movement.

In March 1988, Robin Semer, a staff member of CRTFCA, suggested that media attention to the sanctuary movement had diminished. She predicted that the sanctuary movement will "exist but not flourish." When most social movements fade from public consciousness, donations to movement organizations decrease, and as a result, the social movement wanes (McFarland 1983).

One feature of the sanctuary movement that distinguishes it from other social movements and gives it an additional measure of "survivability" is that it is, for the most part, church-based, and thus has a constant source of organizational support. Other social movements, such as the consumer protection movement, tended to wane as public attention came to focus on policy issues and movement organizations began to see their supply of funds diminish. In contrast, religious organizations involved in the sanctuary movement have a constant source of support from members of their congregations who contribute to the religious organizations, and not specifically to support sanctuary goals. Leaders of these religious organizations may continue to press for the goals of the sanctuary movement even after public support for the movement dissipates. Hence, the sanctuary movement is likely to have a semi-perpetual existence, losing impetus not due to a lack of financial and organizational support, but due to a loss of interest on the part of religious leaders.

Secular fringe organizations. Secular fringe organizations share in common with religious fringe organizations a number of characteristics. The first is their adherence to natural law, or moral concepts, over positive law. Second is their willingness to engage in acts ranging from legal conduct to civil disobedience to violent activity that contravenes positive law, in order to advance natural law objectives. These organizations, like their religious counterparts, do not depend heavily on government for financial support. Neither do they depend heavily on contributions from persons and organizations that have benefited from the political and economic system within the United States, such as private foundations, private corporations, business and professional organizations, and wealthy individuals. Instead, secular fringe organizations tend to rely on small budgets; their funds may be donated by individuals who support their objectives. Like religious fringe organizations, their primary objective is to promote policy goals, and not to ensure organizational maintenance. These organizations also play an important role in communicating the ideas of a social movement, though perhaps in a more sporadic fashion than fringe religious organizations. They tend to be disadvantaged relative to their religious counterparts, which have a measure of legitimacy in the United States due to their status as religious organizations.

For example, the objectives of the Civil Rights movement were also advanced by such groups as the Black Panthers and Black Muslim organizations, and members of these organizations were informed by their leadership of the main goals of the movement. However, when these organizations resorted to illegal activity, the response was swift and severe. Within a short time after its formation, for example, the Black Panthers were deprived, due to criminal convictions and official surveillance, of effective leadership. After some time, the Black Panthers abandoned most of their far-reaching goals and came to act much like a social welfare agency. Although their independence from the government and entrenched interests provided the Black Panthers with the ability to engage in unconventional conduct and support unpopular policy positions, this independence was also, in part, responsible for their demise.

The sanctuary movement has also been supported by a number of secular fringe organizations, which serve to communicate the major ideas of the movement. These secular fringe organizations, like religious fringe organizations, have a natural law orientation and pursue natural law objectives even when this means that participants violate positive law.

One such fringe secular group is the Pledge of Resistance (POR), which was organized nationwide in 1984 "in response to the escalation of U.S. intervention in the war in Central America" (CRTFCA 1988). The Pledge of Resistance was formed for the purpose of carrying out acts of civil disobedience, aimed at gaining media attention and public support for the goals of the sanctuary movement. Although POR is independent from CRTFCA, CRTFCA coordinates the POR in Chicago. An information pamphlet distributed by CRTFCA in February 1988 discusses the activities of the POR in Chicago:

> The Chicago Pledge of Resistance has done numerous creative actions. It has organized against the passage of contra aid, the bombings in El Salvador and U.S. government and press disinformation on Central America; presently, it is organizing around stopping the deployment of the Illinois National Guard to Central America. At the same time, the Pledge responds to emergencies as they occur.

Some of the "creative actions" engaged in by the Chicago POR include a March 1985 sit-in at Illinois Senator Alan J. Dixon's office after he voted in favor of contra aid; nine members of the POR were arrested. Also in March 1985, the Chicago POR conducted a month-long vigil in the Federal Plaza with flowerpots dedicated to persons "martyred" in Central America. In September 1985, members of the Chicago POR demonstrated against U.S. involvement in El Salvador by appearing inside a U.S. Air Force recruiting station in Chicago; five were arrested. In November 1985, members of the Chicago POR staged a mock trial and prayer service in support of 11 sanctuary workers involved in the "Tucson trial"; 200 persons entered the federal building in Chicago and 40 remained, risking arrest (*Basta* December 1985: 3–5).

The Pledge of Resistance is committed to civil disobedience through a concern for natural law principles, namely, to "halt the death and destruction which U.S. military action causes the people of Central America" (CRTFCA 1988). The Pledge of Resistance has opened offices throughout the United States. Its acts of civil disobedience have met with official reaction in the form of arrests, indictments, and criminal convictions. It is too early to say whether the POR will have a significant impact on public opinion relating to U.S. policy toward El Salvador and Guatemala, and refugees from these countries. However, the POR, as a secular fringe organization, is likely to have less impact on public perceptions and policy than religious fringe organizations active in the sanctuary movement, due to the fact that the POR lacks an established communications system that religious organizations typically have, as well as the organizational and financial resources and inherent legitimacy of religious fringe organizations. The POR will probably have a shorter lifespan than will religious fringe organizations active in the sanctuary movement.

Entrenched Organizations

Entrenched organizations were distinguished above from fringe organizations on the basis of the former's adherence to positive law precepts, as opposed to natural law precepts, which are the domain of fringe organizations. Entrenched organizations are, in a very meaningful way, a part of the political system in which they operate and dependent on the status quo. Their financial support is garnered from government and private corporations, business and professional organizations, private foundations, wealthy contributors—individuals and groups that have an interest in maintaining the current political and economic environment.

As a result, entrenched organizations are quite conscious of their reputations and avoid taking unpopular policy positions or engaging in conduct that contravenes positive law. Their link to the political system defines their strategies and actions, which are for the most part set by political and economic structures. For example, entrenched organizations engage in providing social and legal services, and utilize conventional modes of altering public policy. Entrenched organizations, unlike fringe organizations, are primarily committed to organizational maintenance. Typically, entrenched organizations are not the first groups to communicate the ideas of a social movement. This task is left, instead, to fringe organizations. Entrenched organizations only come to support the major ideas of a social movement after those ideas have gained popular attention and, perhaps, support from the public or political entrepreneurs.

There are two major types of entrenched organizations: those that provide social services and those that provide legal services.

Entrenched Organizations that Provide Social Services. The category of entrenched organizations that provide social services includes organizations such as the United Way and the United States Catholic Conference. They are entrenched due to their dependence on grants from federal, state, and local governments and due to the generally cooperative arrangements they have entered into with government. This category of social services providers includes both secular and religious organizations, but the groups share in common a commitment to positive law, to acting in a legal and, for the most part, uncontroversial manner.

Organizations such as these have not become meaningfully involved in the sanctuary movement, except indirectly. They may supply social services to refugees from Central America who have found refuge in a sanctuary in the United States, but this is not an organizational objective. These organizations do not actively engage in communicating the ideas of the sanctuary movement; nor do they act as advocates of those Central America refugees they serve.

Entrenched Organizations That Provide Legal Services. Entrenched organizations that provide legal services share most of the characteristics of entrenched organizations that provide social services. They are dependent on maintenance of the status quo because they obtain their financial resources to a great extent from entrenched interests, including federal, state, and local government, bar associations, business organizations, private foundations, law schools, and wealthy individuals. Their main loyalty is to positive law, even when it conflicts with natural law precepts. Hence, action pursued by these organizations tends to be uniformly legal. The tendency toward legality is even more pronounced in entrenched organizations that offer legal services. Their main activity—

litigation—negates the possibility of extra-legal conduct. Social movements, such as the sanctuary movement, that rely to a great extent on extra-legal conduct and whose adherents claim that the legal system does not provide relief threaten the existence of legal organizations. In fact, such social movements are often justified on the basis that the legal system is largely unresponsive to the ideas of the social movement or the individuals represented by the social movement. An implication is that legal interest groups thus serve no legitimate function, aside from preserving the status quo.

Because entrenched legal interest groups are primarily interested in organizational maintenance and not in effecting major changes in public policy, it is not surprising that a natural antipathy often arises between entrenched legal interest groups and participants in social movements. For example, most (37, or 64 percent) of the 59 legal interest groups interviewed in 1988 that provide services to aliens who seek political asylum or withholding of deportation indicated that they had no interaction whatsoever with persons in the sanctuary movement in spite of the fact that they regularly represent Central Americans who seek asylum and withholding (Yarnold 1990b). Some of the organizational representatives even expressed outright hostility toward the sanctuary movement, indicating that they encourage refugees from Central America to attempt to obtain relief through the legal system, rather than through the illegal mechanism of sanctuary. This is surprising, given the fact that few, if any, of these organizations indicated that they have significant success in representing Central American refugees before the immigration bureaucracy. There was, however, a group of entrenched legal services interest groups (21, or 36 percent of the sample) that is less entrenched or established than others and indicated that they cooperate to some extent with members of the sanctuary movement through, for example, providing legal representation to Central American refugees referred by sanctuary churches or by helping sanctuary churches obtain the release of Central American refugees held in detention facilities. One such organization was Proyecto Libertad, located in Harlingen, Texas. It is interesting to note that entrenched legal organizations that did have contact with the sanctuary movement tended to be younger, less established, and less well known than legal services organizations that never had contact with the sanctuary movement. In addition, legal services organizations that had contact with the sanctuary movement tended to be less stable financially than those with no such contact, depending to a greater extent on donations from churches, and uncertain about the source and existence of future funding (Yarnold 1990b).

It should be noted, however, that even those entrenched legal organizations that had contact with the sanctuary movement did not abandon their commitment to seeking only legal channels of relief for Central American refugees. This is not to say, of course, that entrenched organizations never promote movement goals or communicate these goals. Freeman (1975) shows that although groups within the women's liberation movement were often divided, radical feminist groups and more conservative groups such as Women's Equity Action League (WEAL) worked together toward a movement goal of promoting women's equality and also served to communicate the ideas of the movement.

The relationship between entrenched legal interest groups and fringe sanctuary organizations in the refugee/asylum policy area is somewhat exceptional. Fringe organizations within the sanctuary movement, by placing primary emphasis on illegal assistance to refugees and asylees, directly challenge the legitimacy of entrenched legal interest groups.

Nevertheless, entrenched groups are limited in their advocacy of policy goals by the fact that they are dependent on other entrenched interests and perhaps the government for their support. If they take a policy position that is too divergent from those taken by organizations that support them, these entrenched organizations will likely lose their support. Hence, in deciding between an unpopular policy position and ensuring organizational maintenance, entrenched organizations that continue to exist have likely favored organizational maintenance. Not surprisingly, entrenched legal organizations do not serve as effective communicators of the major ideas of the sanctuary movement.

A Second Link between Organized Interest Groups and Social Movements: Proliferation of Interest Groups

Another important aspect of social movements relates to their ability to increase countervailing power through the proliferation of interest groups in the course of a movement (McFarland 1987; Freeman 1975).

The sanctuary movement, for example, has coincided with an increase in interest groups that assist refugees from Central America. The Central America Resource Center in Austin, Texas, has published since 1984 a *Directory of Central America Organizations*, consisting of a list of organizations that offer assistance to Central American refugees nationwide.

The 1984 edition of the *Directory* lists 400 to 425 Central American organizations; the 1985 *Directory* lists 850 organizations; by 1987 (third edition), 1,070 Central American organizations were included in the *Directory* (Central American Resource Center 1984, 1985, 1987). The Central American organizations are grouped into the following categories: refugee legal assistance, refugee sanctuary, research, solidarity, speakers, and travel. In each year since the *Directory* was issued, the number of organizations in each category has increased. This provides indirect support for the hypothesis that the sanctuary movement has led to the formation of new interest groups that provide legal services, social services, advocacy, and sanctuary to Central American refugees.

Earlier in this analysis, the increase in the number of sanctuary locations for refugees from Central America was also noted, from 30 in 1982 to 448 in December 1987. Most of these were made available by religious organizations, and the simultaneous mobilization of secular fringe organizations including, for example, the Pledge of Resistance.

The 59 entrenched legal services organizations mentioned earlier are also instructive. Most of the organizations that assisted aliens in asylum-related appeals to the BIA and the federal courts are relatively new organizations, formed in or after 1980 (Yarnold 1990b).

The theoretical importance of the fact that the sanctuary movement spawned the growth of new interest groups is that in doing so, it also served to increase countervailing power against the U.S. policy of barring the entry of Salvadoran and Guatemalan refugees, and in denying that these aliens are political, and not economic, refugees.

Countervailing power produced by social movements tends to decrease when social movements wane, and public support for the movement and movement organizations diminishes. However, the sanctuary movement is unusual in that its power may not wane even if public support for sanctuary diminishes, due to the fact that the sanctuary movement is largely the product of religious groups that have the independent financial and organizational resources necessary to sustain the movement even in the absence of popular support.

Conclusion

The sanctuary movement, like social movements generally, was the product of a collective decision on the part of (primarily religious) individuals and groups in favor of natural law precepts over positive law when the two were in conflict. U.S. refugee and asylum policy, or positive law, serves to limit immigration flows and to favor in refugee admissions aliens from hostile countries of origin. Individuals and fringe organizations in the United States chose to follow natural law precepts and violate positive law by sheltering Central American refugees in the U.S. in violation of the law. Fringe religious and secular organizations carried the sanctuary movement forward with little direct assistance from entrenched organizations in the United States, which rely for their support on other entrenched interests and government. Fringe sanctuary organizations, which based their resort to illegal channels on the illegitimacy of political and legal structures in the United States, directly challenge the existence of entrenched legal interest groups. Entrenched organizations were not particularly effective in communicating the ideas of the sanctuary movement.

The sanctuary movement also seemed to spawn new interest groups dedicated to assisting refugees and asylees. The U.S. policy of limiting immigration flows and favoring hostile-state aliens thus led to a countermobilization of public interest groups oriented toward helping refugees and asylees. These groups operate both within and outside the parameters of the legal system.

Bibliography

Abu Eain v. Wilkes, 641 F.2d 504 (7th Cir. 1981).

Aldrich, J., and C. Cnudde. 1975. "Probing the Bounds of Conventional Wisdom: A Comparison of Regression, Probit, and Discriminant Analysis." *American Journal of Political Science* 19: 571–608.

Allen, F. A. 1981. "Legal Values and the Rehabilitative Ideal." In *Sentencing*, H. Gross and A. Von Hirsch, eds., pp. 110–117. New York: Oxford University Press.

Appleton, S. F. 1981. "Beyond the Limits of Reproductive Choice." *Columbia Law Review* 81 (4): 721–58.

Arthur D. Little, Inc. 1980. "Determinate and Indeterminate Sentence Law Comparison Study: Feasibility of Adapting Law to a Sentencing Commission-Guidance Approach." San Francisco: Arthur D. Little.

Austin, T. L. 1980. "The Influence of Legal and Extra-Legal Factors on Sentencing Dispositions in Rural, Semi-Rural and Urban Counties." Ann Arbor, MI: University Microfilms International.

Bardach, E. 1984. *The Implementation Game*. Cambridge: The MIT Press.

Bassiouni, M. C. 1983. *International Extradition*. New York: Oceana Publications.

Basta, National Newsletter of the Chicago Religious Task Force on Central America. December 1985.

———. June 1986.

———. September 1986.

———. December 1986.

———. June 1987.

———. December 1987.

Baum, L. 1989. *The Supreme Court*. Washington, D.C.: Congressional Quarterly.

Beiser, E. N. 1978. "The Rhode Island Supreme Court: A Well-Integrated Political System." In *American Court Systems*, S. Goldman and A. Sarat, eds., pp. 470–79. San Francisco: W. H. Freeman and Co.

Blank, R. H. 1984. "Judicial Decision Making and Biological Fact: Roe v. Wade and the Unresolved Question of Fetal Viability." *Western Political Quarterly* 37: 584–602.

Blum, C. 1986. "The Ninth Circuit and the Protection of Asylum Since the Passage of the Refugee Act of 1980." *San Diego Law Review* 23: 327–73.

Bolce, L. 1988. "Abortion and Presidental Elections: The Impact of Public Perceptions of Party and Candidate Positions." *Presidential Studies Quarterly* 18: 815–29.

Bowker, L. H. 1978. *Women, Crime, and the Criminal Justice System.* Lexington, MA: Lexington Books.

Briggs, V. 1984. *Immigration Policy and the American Labor Force.* Baltimore: Johns Hopkins University Press.

Burek, D. M., K. E. Koek, and A. Novallo, eds. 1989. *Encyclopedia of Associations 1990.* 24th edition, vol. 1. Detroit: Gale Research Inc.

Burton, W. L. 1988. *Melting Pot Soldiers.* Ames, IA: Iowa State University Press.

Byrne, S. 1969. *Irish Emigration to the United States.* New York: Arno Press and New York Times.

Caldeira, G. 1981. "Judicial Incentives." In *Courts, Law, and Judicial Processes,* S. S. Ulmer, eds., pp. 143–49. New York: Free Press.

———. 1987. "Public Opinion and the U.S. Supreme Court: FDR's Court-packing Plan." *American Political Science Review* 81: 1139–54.

Carp, R., and C. Rowland. 1983. *Policy Making and Politics in the Federal District Courts.* Knoxville: University of Tennessee Press.

Carrington, D. 1974. "U.S. Appeals in Civil Cases: A Field and Statistical Study." *Houston Law Review* 11: 1101–29.

Carroll, J., W. Perkowitz, A. Lurigio, and F. Weaver. 1987. "Sentencing Goals, Causal Attributions, Ideology, and Personality." *Journal of Personality and Social Psychology* 52(1): 107–18.

Carter, L. H. 1983. *Administrative Law and Politics.* Boston: Little, Brown and Co.

Casper, J. D. 1981. "The Public Defender: Man in the Middle." In *Courts, Law, and Judicial Processes,* S. S. Ulmer, ed., pp. 87–94. New York: Free Press.

Catholic Agitator. August 1984.

Center for American Woman and Politics (CAWP), National Information Bank on Women in Public Office (NIB), Eagleton Institute of Politics, Rutgers University, New Jersey.

Central America Resource Center. 1984. *Directory of Central America Organizations.* Austin, Texas.

———. 1985. *Directory of Central America Organizations.* Austin, Texas.

———. *Directory of Central America Organizations.* Austin, Texas.

Chiswick, B. R. 1981. "Guidelines for the Reform of Immigration Policy." In *Essays in Contemporary Economic Problems: Demand, Productivity, and Population,* ed. the American Enterprise Institute for Public Policy Research, pp. 309–47. Washington, D.C.

———. 1986. "Is the New Immigration Less Skilled Than the Old?" *Journal of Labor Economics* 4: 165–92.

Chomsky, N. 1983. *The Fateful Triangle.* Boston: South End Press.

Clarke, A. 1987. "Moral Protest, Status Defense and the Anti-Abortion Campaign." *British Journal of Sociology* 38: 235–53.

Cockburn, A. 1989. "Aborted Justice." *New Statesman & Society* 2: 19–20, July 14, 1989.

Combs, M. W., and S. Welch. 1982. "Blacks, Whites, and Attitudes Toward Abortion." *Public Opinion Quarterly* 46: 510–20.

Congressional Quarterly. 1988. *Congress A to Z*. Washington, DC: Congressional Quarterly.

———. 1973–1990. *Congressional Quarterly Almanac*. Washington, DC: Congressional Quarterly, vols. 29–45.

Cook, B. B. 1977. "Public Opinion and Federal Judicial Policy." *Journal of Political Science* 2: 567–600.

———. 1981. "Sentencing Behavior of Federal Judges—Draft Cases—1972." In S. Ulmer, ed., *Courts, Law, and Judicial Processes*, pp. 462–69. New York: Free Press.

Cook, B. B., L. F. Goldstein, K. O'Connor, and S. M. Talarico. 1988. *Women in the Judicial Process*. Washington, DC: American Political Science Association.

Cooper, C., D. Kelley, and S. Larson. 1982. "Judicial and Executive Discretion in the Sentencing Process: Analysis of State Felony Code Provisions." Washington, DC: American University, Washington College of Law.

Council of State Governments. 1987. *State Elective Officials and the Legislatures 1987–1988*. Lexington: Council of State Governments.

Crites, L. L. and W. L. Hepperle, eds. 1987. *Women, the Courts, and Equality*. Beverly Hills: Sage Publications.

CRTFCA. 1988. *Information Pamphlet*. Chicago: Chicago Religious Task Force on Central America.

Cummings, M. C., Jr., and David Wise. 1985. *Democracy Under Pressure*. San Diego: Harcourt Brace Jovanovich.

Daly, K. 1987. "Discrimination in the Criminal Courts: Family, Gender, and the Problem of Equal Treatment." *Social Forces* 66(1): 152–75.

Damas, R. Y. 1986. "To Return the Persecuted to the Source, the Origin, the Cause of Their Suffering is an Act of Injustice in the Eyes of Christian Love." *Basta* (December): 24–25.

Danelski, D. J. 1978. "The Influence of the Chief Justice in the Decisional Process of the Supreme Court." In *American Court Systems*, S. Goldman and A. Sarat, eds., pp. 506–19. San Francisco: W. H. Freeman and Co.

———. 1981. "Values as Variables in Judicial Decision Making." In *Courts, Law, And Judicial Processes*, S. S. Ulmer, ed., pp. 397–402. New York: Free Press.

Davidson, R. H., and W. J. Oleszek. 1981. *Congress and Its Members*. Washington, DC: Congressional Quarterly Press.

Dawson, R. O. 1969. *Sentencing: The Decision as to Type, Length and Conditions of Sentence*. Boston: Little, Brown.

Department of Corrections. 1988. "Report of the Overcrowding Task Force." Department of Corrections, State of Vermont, November 17.

Doe v. Bolton, 410 U.S. 179 (1973).

Dolbeare, K. M. 1978. "The Federal District Courts and Urban Public Policy." In *American Court Systems*, S. Goldman and A. Sarat, eds., pp. 535–545. San Francisco: W. H. Freeman and Co.

Dornette, W. S., and R. R. Cross. 1986. *Federal Judiciary Almanac 1986*. New York: John Wiley & Sons.

Downs, A. 1957. *An Economic Theory of Democracy*. New York: Harper.

Dudley, R. L. 1989. "State High Court Decision Making in Pornography Cases." Prepared for the 1989 annual meeting of the American Political Science Association, Atlanta, Georgia.

Dye, T. R. 1966. *Politics, Economics, and the Public: Policy Outcomes in the American States*. Chicago: Rand McNally and Co.

Eagleton, C. 1957. *International Government*. New York: Ronald Press Co.

Easton, D. 1965. *The Political System*. New York: Knopf.

Economist, The. 1989. "The Fearful Politics of Abortion." 312 (July 8): 21–23.

Edwards, C. 1981. *Hugo Grotius, the Miracle of Holland*. Chicago: Nelson Hall.

Edwards, C. L. 1983. "Political Asylum and Withholding of Deportation: Defining the Appropriate Standard of Proof Under the Refugee Act of 1980." *San Diego Law Review* 21: 171–84.

Elazar, D. 1972. *American Federalism: A View from the States*. New York: Thomas Y. Crowell Co.

Engel, M. 1985. *State and Local Politics*. New York: St. Martin's Press.

Epstein, L. 1985. *Conservatives in Court*. Knoxville: University of Tennessee Press.

Extradition Act of U.S., 18 U.S.C. 3184–3190; as amended November 18, 1988, P.L. 100–690, Title VII, Subtitle B, Section 7087, 102 Stat. 4409.

Farrell, M. 1985. *Sheltering the Fugitive?* Dublin, Ireland: Mercier Press.

Forst, M. L. 1982. *Sentencing Reform*. Beverly Hills: Sage Publications.

Frank, J. 1978. "Facts Are Guesses." In *American Court Systems*, S. Goldman and A. Sarat, eds., pp. 310–16. San Francisco: W. H. Freeman and Co.

Frankel, M. E. 1973. *Criminal Sentences*. New York: Hill and Wang.

Franklin, C. H., and L. C. Kosaki. 1989. "Republican Schoolmaster: The U.S. Supreme Court, Public Opinion, and Abortion." *American Political Science Review* 83: 751–71.

Freeman, J. 1975. *The Politics of Women's Liberation*. Chicago: University of Chicago Press.

Galanter, M. 1974. "Why the 'Haves' Come Out Ahead: Speculation on the Limits of Social Change." *Law and Society Review* 9: 85–160.

———. 1978. "Who Wins?" In *American Court Systems*, S. Goldman and A. Sarat, eds., pp. 529–34. San Francisco: W. H. Freeman and Co.

Garraty, J. A. 1987. *Quarrels That Have Shaped The Constitution*. New York: Harper & Row.

Gibson, J. L. 1977. "Discriminant Functions, Role Orientations and Judicial Behavior: Theoretical and Methodological Linkages." *Journal of Politics* 37: 917–36.

Giles, M. W., and T. G. Walker. 1978. "Judicial Policy-Making and Southern School Segregation." In *American Court Systems*, S. Goldman and A. Sarat, eds., pp. 386–95. San Francisco: W. H. Freeman and Co.

Glick, H. R. 1983. *Courts, Politics and Justice*. New York: McGraw-Hill, Inc.

Golden, R., and M. McConnell. 1986. *Sanctuary: The New Underground Railroad*. New York: Orbis Books.

Goldman, S. 1975. "Voting Behavior on the U.S. Court of Appeals." *American Political Science Review* 69: 491–506.

———. 1978. "Voting Behavior on the United States Courts of Appeals Revisited." In *American Court Systems*, S. Goldman and A. Sarat, eds., pp. 396–411. San Francisco: W. H. Freeman and Co.

Goldstein, J. 1986. "The Political Economy of Trade: Institutions of Protection." *American Political Science Review* 80: 161–84.

Gottfredson, D. M. 1981. "Sentencing Guidelines." In *Sentencing*, H. Gross and A. Von Hirsch, eds., pp. 310–14. New York: Oxford University Press.

Gottfredson, D. M., L. Wilkins, and P. Hoffman. 1981. "Policy Implications of Guidelines." In *Sentencing*, H. Gross and A. Von Hirsch, eds., pp. 315–17. New York: Oxford University Press.

Gottfredson, M. R., and D. M. Gottfredson. 1980. *Decisionmaking in Criminal Justice*. Cambridge: Ballinger.

Graber, M. A. 1990. "Interpreting Abortion." Prepared for the 1990 annual meeting of the American Political Science Association, San Francisco, August 30–September 2, 1990.

Graeber, D. 1973. "Judicial Activity and Public Attitude." *Buffalo Law Review* 23: 465–97.

Granberg, D. 1985. "An Anomaly in Political Perception." *Public Opinion Quarterly* 49: 504–16.

Griswold, D. 1986. "Deviation from Sentencing Guidelines: The Issue of Unwarranted Disparity." *Journal of Criminal Justice* 15: 317–29.

Griswold v. Connecticut, 381 U.S. 479 (1965).

Gross, H., and A. Von Hirsch. 1981. *Sentencing*. New York: Oxford University Press.

Gryski, G. S., E. C. Main, and W. J. Dixon. 1986. "Models of State Court High Decision Making in Sex Discrimination Cases." *Journal of Politics* 48: 143–55.

Hagan, J. 1975. "Law, Order and Sentencing: A Study of Attitude in Action." *Sociometry* 38: 347.

———. 1987. "Review Essay: A Great Truth in the Study of Crime." *Criminology* 25(2): 421–28.

Haire, S., and D. R. Songer. 1990. "A Multivariate Model of Voting on the United States Courts of Appeals." Prepared for the 1990 annual meeting of the Midwest Political Science Association, Chicago, April 7, 1990.

Hall, J. A. 1987. "A Recommended Approach to Bail in International Extradition Cases." *Michigan Law Review* 86: 599.

Harris, D. 1967. "The Right to a Fair Trial in Criminal Proceedings as a Human Right." *International and Comparative Law Quarterly* 16: 352–78.

Heclo, H. 1978. "Issue Networks and the Executive Establishment." In *The New American Political System*, A. King, ed., pp. 161–85. Washington, DC: American Enterprise Institute.

Helton, A. C. 1984. "Political Asylum Under the 1980 Refugee Act: An Unfulfilled Promise." *University of Michigan Law Reference* 17: 243–64.

———. 1985. "The Proper Role of Discretion in Political Asylum Determinations." *San Diego Law Review* 22: 999–1020.

Higgins, R. 1963. *The Development of International Law through the Political Organs of the United Nations*. New York: Oxford University Press.

Hildreth, A. and E. M. Dran. 1990. "How Women Define Women's Interests: Abortion and Gender Mobilization in Illinois." Paper presented at the annual meeting of the Midwest Political Science Association, Chicago, April 6, 1990.

Hofferbert, R. I. 1974. *The Study of Public Policy*. New York: Bobbs-Merrill Co.

Horan, D. J. 1981. "Critical Abortion Litigation." *Catholic Lawyer* 26: 178–208.

Howard J. W., Jr. 1978. "Role Perceptions and Behavior in Three U.S. Courts of Appeals." In *American Court Systems*, S. Goldman and A. Sarat, eds., pp. 480–89. San Francisco: W. H. Freeman and Co.

Hyndman, P. 1986. "Refugee under International Law with a Reference to the Concept of Asylum." *Australian Law Journal* 60: 148–55.

Illinois Criminal Sexual Assault Act. 1984.

International City Management Association. 1989. *The Municipal Yearbook 1989.* Washington, DC: ICMA.

Jacob, H. 1981. "Attorneys for the Public." In *Courts, Law, and Judicial Processes*, S. S. Ulmer, ed., pp. 82–87. New York: Free Press.

Johnson, S. D., J. B. Tamney, and R. Burton. 1990. "The Abortion Controversy: Conflicting Beliefs and Values in American Society." Prepared for the 1990 annual meeting of the American Political Science Association, San Francisco, August 30–September 2, 1990.

Judicial Conference. 1983. *Judges Of The United States*, 2nd ed. Published under the auspices of the Bicentennial Committee of the Judicial Conference of the United States. Washington, DC: U.S. Government Printing Office.

Karadzole v. Artukovic, 247 F.2d 198 (9th Cir. 1957) and *United States ex rel. Karadzole v. Artukovic*, 170 F.Supp. 383 (S.D. Cal. 1959).

Kemp, K. A., R. A. Carp, and D. W. Brady. 1978. "The Supreme Court and Social Change: The Case of Abortion." *Western Political Quarterly* 31: 19–31.

Kester, J. G. 1988. "Some Myths of United States Extradition Law." *Georgetown Law Journal* 76: 1441.

Krasner, S. D. 1978. *Defending the National Interest*. Princeton: Princeton University Press.

Kritzer, H. 1978. "Political Correlates of the Behavior of Federal District Judges." *Journal of Politics* 40: 25–57.

LaFree, G. D. 1989. *Rape and Criminal Justice*. Belmont, CA: Wadsworth.

Lawson, K. 1984. "Sex Crimes: Revised." *Illinois Issues* (February): 6–11.

Legge, J. S., Jr. 1983. "The Determinants of Attitudes Toward Abortion in the American Electorate." *Western Political Science Quarterly* 36: 479–90.

Levin, M. A. 1978. "Urban Politics and Judicial Behavior." In *American Court Systems*, S. Goldman and A. Sarat, eds., pp. 338–47. San Francisco: W. H. Freeman and Co.

Lineberry, R., and I. Sharkansky. 1978. *Urban Politics and Public Policy*. New York: Harper & Row.

Lipsky, M. 1980. *Street Level Bureaucrats*. New York: Sage Publications.

Loder, T. 1986. *No One but Us*. San Diego: Luramedia.

Loescher, G., and J. A. Scanlan. 1986. *Calculated Kindness*. New York: Free Press.

Lofland, J. 1969. *Deviance and Identity*. Prentice-Hall.

Lowi, T. M., Jr. 1979. *The End of Liberalism*. New York: W. W. Norton and Co.

Luker, K. 1984. *Abortion and the Politics of Motherhood*. Berkeley: University of California Press.

Madison, C. 1989. "Arab-American Lobby Fights Rearguard Battle to Influence U.S. Mideast Policy." In *Readings in American Government and Politics*, Randall P. Ripley and Elliot E. Slotnick, eds., pp. 331–39. New York: McGraw-Hill.

Margolis, M., and K. Neary. 1980. "Pressure Politics Revisited: The Anti-Abortion Campaign." *Policy Studies Journal* 8(5): 698–716.

Mashaw, J. L. 1985. *Due Process in the Administrative State*. New Haven: Yale University Press.

Mazmanian, D. A., and P. A. Sabatier. 1983. *Implementation and Public Policy.*

Glenview, IL: Scott, Foresman and Co.

McConnell, G. 1966. *Private Power and American Democracy*. New York: Knopf.

———. 1986. "Bringing the War Home." *Basta* (June): 7–14.

McFarland, A. S. 1980. *Public Interest Lobbies*. Washington, D.C.: American Enterprise Institute for Public Policy Research.

———. 1983. "Public Interest Lobbies versus Minority Faction." In *Interest Group Politics*, A. J. Cigler and B. A. Loomis, eds., pp. 324–53. Washington, DC: Congressional Quarterly Press.

———. 1987. "Interest Groups and Theories of Power in America." *British Journal of Political Science* 17: 129–47.

Michigan Department of Corrections. 1988. *Annual Report*. Lansing, MI: Michigan Department of Corrections.

Miethe, T. 1987. "Charging and Plea Bargaining Practices under Determinate Sentences: An Investigation of the Hydraulic Displacement of Discretion." *Journal of Criminal Law and Criminology* 78: 155–76.

Miller, W., and D. Stokes. 1963. "Constituency Influence in Congress." *American Journal of Political Science* 57: 45–56.

Montana Code Annotated. 1988. Helena: Montana Legislative Council.

Morris, H. 1981. "Persons and Punishment." In *Sentencing*, H. Gross and A. Von Hirsch, eds., pp. 93–109. New York: Oxford University Press.

Murphy, W. F. 1981. "Courts as Small Groups." In *Courts, Law, and Judicial Processes*, S. S. Ulmer, ed., pp. 363–67. New York: Free Press.

Myers, M. 1987. "Economic Inequality and Discrimination in Sentencing." *Social Forces*: 65(3): 746–66.

———. 1988. "Social Background and the Sentencing Behavior of Judges." *Criminology* 26(4): 649–73.

Nagel, I., and J. Hagan. 1983. "Gender and Crime: Offense Patterns and Criminal Court Sanctions." *Crime and Justice: Annual Review of Research* 4: 91–144.

Nagel, S. S. 1961. "Political Party Affiliation and Judges' Decisions." *American Political Science Review* 55: 843–50.

National Lawyers Guild. 1986. *Central America Refugee Defense Fund Newsletter*. June 6, 1986.

Newman, D. J. 1972. "Perspectives of Probation: Legal Issues and Professional Trends." In *The Challenge of Change in the Correctional Process*, pp. 7–8. Hackensack, NJ: National Council on Crime and Delinquency.

Newman, D. J., and P. R. Anderson. 1989. *Introduction to Criminal Justice*. New York: Random House.

Noonan, J. 1979. *A Private Choice: Abortion in America in the Seventies*. New York: Free Press.

O'Connor, K. 1980. *Women's Organizations' Use of the Courts*. Lexington: Lexington Books.

O'Leary, V., M. Gottfredson, and A. Gelman. 1975. "Contemporary Sentencing Proposals." *Criminal Law Bulletin* 11: 555–86.

Olson, M. 1971. *The Logic of Collective Action*. Boston: Harvard University Press.

Page, B. I., R. T. Shapiro, P. W. Gronke, and R. M. Rosenberg. 1984. "Constituency, Party, and Representation in Congress." *Public Opinion Quarterly* 48: 741–56.

Parker, K. 1985. "Human Rights and Humanitarian Law." *Whittier Law Review* 7: 675–81.

Petchesky, R. 1981. "Antiabortion, Antifeminism and the Rise of the New Right." *Feminist Studies* 7(2): 206–46.

———. 1984. *Abortion and Woman's Choice*. New York: Longman.

Peterson, R., and J. Hagan. 1984. "Changing Conceptions of Race: Towards an Account of Anomalous Findings of Sentencing Research." *American Sociological Review* 49: 56–70.

Pindyck, R., and D. Rubinfeld. 1981. *Econometric Models and Econometric Forecasts*. New York: McGraw-Hill.

Pious, R. 1979. *The American Presidency*. New York: Basic Books.

Preston, R. K. 1986. "Asylum Adjudications: Do State Department Advisory Opinions Violate Refugees' Rights and United States International Obligations?" *Maryland Law Review* 45: 91–140.

Pritchett, C. H. 1978. "Voting Behavior on the United States Supreme Court." In *American Court Systems*, S. Goldman and A. Sarat, eds., pp. 424–31. San Francisco: W. H. Freeman and Co.

Quinn v. Robinson, No. C–82–6688 PPA (N.D. Cal. 1983). Refugee Act of 1980, Public Law No. 96–212, 96th Cong., 2nd Sess., March 17, 1980.

Richardson, R. J., and K. N. Vines. 1978. "Judicial Constituencies: The Politics of Structure." In *American Court Systems*, S. Goldman and A. Sarat, eds., pp. 348–53. San Francisco: W. H. Freeman and Co.

Ripley, R. B., and E. E. Slotnick, 1989. *Readings in American Government and Politics*. New York: McGraw-Hill.

Robinson, J., and G. Smith. 1981. "The Effectiveness of Correctional Programs." In *Sentencing*, H. Gross and A. Von Hirsch, eds., pp. 118–29. New York: Oxford University Press.

Roe v. Wade, 410 U.S. 113 (1973).

Rosenne, S. 1973. *The World Court*. Dobbs Ferry, NY: A. W. Sijthoff-Leiden, Oceana Publications.

Rothman, D. J. 1981. "Decarcerating Prisoners and Patients." In *Sentencing*, H. Gross and A. Von Hirsch, eds., pp. 130–47. New York: Oxford University Press.

Sackett, V. A. 1985. "Between Pro-Life and Pro-Choice." *Public Opinion* 8 (April/May): 53–55.

Schattschneider, E. E. 1960. *The Semisovereign People*. New York: Holt, Reinhart and Winston.

Schubert, G. 1965. *The Judicial Mind*. Evanston, IL: Northwestern University Press.

Schur, E. 1971. *Labeling Deviant Behavior: Its Sociological Implications*. New York: Harper & Row.

Scott, J. 1987. *Conflicting Values and Compromise Beliefs about Abortion*. Doctoral dissertation, University of Michigan, University Microfilms International.

Scott, J., and H. Schuman. 1988. "Attitude Strength and Social Action in the Abortion Dispute." *American Sociological Review* 53: 785–93.

Segal, J. 1984. "Predicting Supreme Court Cases Probabilistically: The Search and Seizure Cases 1962–1981." *American Political Science Review* 78: 891–900.

———. 1985. "Measuring Change on the Supreme Court: Examining Alternative Models." *American Journal of Political Science* 29: 461–79.

Segers, M. C. 1982. "Can Congress Settle the Abortion Issue?" *Hastings Center Report* 12(2): 20–28.

Simon, H. A. 1957. *Administrative Behavior*. New York: Macmillan.

Simon, H. A., D. W. Smithburg, and V. A. Thompson. 1962. *Public Administration.* New York: Knopf.

Sobrino, J. 1987. "Theological Analysis of the Sanctuary Movement." *Basta* (June): 19–24.

Spaeth, H. J. 1981. "The Attitudes and Values of Supreme Court Justices." In *Courts, Law, and Judicial Processes*, S. S. Ulmer, ed., pp. 387–97. New York: Free Press.

Spencer, C. C. 1978. "Sexual Assault: The Second Victimization." In *Women, the Courts, and Equality*, L. Crites and W. Hepperle, eds., pp. 135–54. Beverly Hills: Sage Publications.

Spohn, C., J. Gruhl, and S. Welch. 1981–82. "The Effects of Race on Sentencing: A Re-Examination of an Unsettled Question." *Law and Society Review* 16(1): 71–88.

Sprague, J. D. 1968. *Voting Patterns of the U.S. Supreme Court.* New York: Bobbs-Merrill Co.

State of Montana Supreme Court. 1988. *Montana Courts: 1988 Judicial Report.* Helena, MT.

Steel, R. D. 1985. *Steel on Immigration Law.* San Francisco: Bancroft-Whitney Co.

Steffensmeier, D., and J. H. Kramer. 1982. "Sex-Based Differences in the Sentencing of Adult Criminal Defendants: An Empirical Test and Theoretical Overview." *Sociology and Social Research: An International Journal* 66(3): 289–304.

Stokes, D. 1963. "Spatial Models of Party Competition." *American Political Science Review* 57: 368–77.

Tanenhaus, J. 1961. "Supreme Court Attitudes Toward Federal Administrative Agencies 1947–1956—An Application of Social Science Methods to the Study of Judicial Process." *Vanderbilt Law Review* 14: 482–501.

Tanenhaus, J., M. Schick, M. Muraskin, and D. Rosen. 1981. "The Supreme Court's Certiorari Jurisdiction: Cue Theory." In *Courts, Law, and Judicial Processes*, S. Ulmer, ed., pp. 273–83. New York: Free Press.

Tatalovich, R., and B. W. Daynes. 1981. *The Politics of Abortion.* New York: Praeger.

Turk, A. 1969. *Criminality and Legal Order.* Chicago: Rand McNally.

———. 1972. *Legal Sanctioning and Social Control.* Washington, DC: Government Printing Office.

Ulmer, S. S. 1981. *Courts, Law, and Judicial Processes.* New York: Free Press.

Ungs, T. D., and L. R. Bass. 1972. "Judicial Role Perceptions: A Q-Technique Study of Ohio Judges." *Law and Society Review* 6: 343–66.

Unnever, J., and L. Hembroff. 1988. "The Prediction of Racial/Ethic Sentencing Disparities: An Expectation States Approach." *Journal of Research in Crime and Delinquency* 25: 53–82.

U.S. Bureau of the Census. 1954. *Seventeenth U.S. Census, Special Reports, Nativity and Parentage*, Vol. 4, Part 3, Ch. A, Table 12, pp. 3A–71–74. Washington, DC: U.S. Government Printing Office.

———. 1975. *Historical Statistics of the United States: Colonial Time to 1970*, Part 1. Washington, DC: U.S. Government Printing Office.

———. 1982. *Statistical Abstract of the United States: 1982–83*. Washington, DC: U.S. Government Printing Office.

———. 1986. *State and Metropolitan Area Data Book.* Washington, DC: U.S. Government Printing Office.

————. 1988. *County and City Data Book.* Washington, DC: U.S. Government Printing Office.

U.S. Department of Justice. 1984. *1984 Statistical Yearbook of the Immigration and Naturalization Service.* Washington, DC: Bureau of Public Affairs.

U.S. Department of Labor. 1980–87. *Employment and Earnings.* Washington, DC: Bureau of Public Affairs.

U.S. Department of State. 1980–87 and 1930–90. *Background Notes.* Washington, DC: Bureau of Public Affairs.

Van Der Hout, M. 1985. "The Politics of Asylum." *California Lawyer* 5: 72(1).

Vines, K. N. 1963. "The Role of Circuit Courts of Appeal in the Federal Judicial Process: A Case Study." *Midwest Journal of Political Science* 7: 305–19.

————. 1978. "Federal District Judges and Race Relation Cases in the South." In *American Court Systems*, S. Goldman and A. Sarat, eds., pp. 376–85. San Francisco: W. H. Freeman and Co.

Von Hirsch, A. 1987. *Past or Future Crimes.* New Brunswick, NJ: Rutgers University Press.

Vose, C. 1959. *Caucasians Only.* Berkeley: Knopf.

Walker, J. L. 1983. "The Origins and Maintenance of Interest Groups in America." *American Political Science Review* 127: 390–406.

Wall, D. 1985. "Michigan Supreme Court and Court of Appeals Election." Paper presented at Midwest Political Science Association, Chicago, Illinois, April.

Wenner, L. M. 1982. *The Environmental Decade in Court.* Bloomington, IN: Indiana University Press.

Wenner, L., and L. Dutter. 1988. "Contextual Influences on Court Outcomes." *Western Political Quarterly* 41: 115–34.

Williams, K., and S. Drake. 1980. "Social Structure, Crime and Criminalization: An Empirical Examination of the Conflict Perspective." *The Sociological Quarterly* 21: 563–75.

Williams, K., and M. Timberlake. 1984. "Structured Inequality, Conflict, and Control: A Cross-National Test of the Threat Hypothesis." *Social Forces* 63: 414–32.

Wolpert, R., and G. N. Rosenberg. 1990. "The Least Dangerous Branch: Market Forces and the Implementation of Roe." Prepared for the American Political Science Association, San Francisco, August 30–September 2.

Woodman, S. 1989. "Reproductive Rights." *New Statesman & Society* 2 (August 18): 20–21.

Yarnold, B. M. 1988. "United States Refugee and Asylum Policy: Factors That Impact Legislative, Administrative and Judicial Decisions." Doctoral dissertation, University of Illinois at Chicago.

————. 1990a. "Federal Court Outcomes in Asylum-Related Appeals 1980–1987: A Highly 'Politicized' Process." *Policy Sciences* 23 (4): 291–306.

————. 1990b. *Refugees without Refuge: Formation and Failed Implementation of U.S. Political Asylum Policy in the 1980s.* Lanham, MD: University Press of America.

————. 1990c. "The Refugee Act of 1980 and the De-Politicization of Refugee/Asylum Admissions: An Example of Failed Policy Implementation." *American Politics Quarterly* 18(4) (October): 527–36.

————. 1991a. *International Fugitives: A New Role for the International Court of Justice.* New York: Praeger.

————. 1991b. "The Role of Religious Organizations in the U.S. Sanctuary Movement,"
     Chapter 3 of *The Role of Religious Organizations in Social Movements*, B. M.
     Yarnold, ed. New York: Praeger.
Zatz, M. 1987. "The Changing Forms of Racial/Ethic Biases in Sentencing." *Journal
     of Research in Crime and Delinquency* 24(1): 69–92.
Zimring, F. 1981. "Making the Punishment Fit the Crime: A Consumers' Guide to
     Sentencing Reform." In *Sentencing*, H. Gross and A. Von Hirsch, eds., pp. 327–
     35. New York: Oxford University Press.

Index

abortion, 55–57, 63–64, 67, 104, 117;
  biological debate, 5; decision, 55;
  federal court outcomes, 64; laws, 62,
  67; limits on, 65; movement, 64; rights,
  66–67
abortion cases, 6, 53, 57–58, 61, 66–
  68, 105
adjudication, 71–73, 86
administrative adjudication, 104
Administrative Appeals Board, 71
administrative decision makers, 12, 71–
  72, 78; and foreign policy goals, 15
administrative decision making, 72, 78
advisory opinions, 78; in asylum cases,
  77; in immigration cases, 15
agencies, 71; and federal court cases, 10,
  43
agency abuses, correction of, 72
agency action, challenges to, 72
agency adjudication, 73–74
ambiguity, policy goals and, 14
American Civil Liberties Union (ACLU),
  62, 86
American Immigration Lawyers' Association, 87
amicus curiae, 8, 23, 43, 45, 58, 73, 78,
  82, 84, 85

Amnesty International, 87
anti-abortion movement, 58, 61–63, 64–
  65, 66, 67, 103
appeals: asylum-related, to federal courts,
  13; interest groups and, 11; judicial, 4
Arab lobby, 47
asylees, 13, 22, 74
asylum, 112, 126; request for, 14; statutory recognition, 74
asylum and witholding, 82, 112; applications for, 76; claims and appeals, 85;
  standards for, 15; vagueness of standards, 15
asylum policy, 11, 74; humanitarian goals
  of, 84
asylum-related appeals, 6, 10, 11, 17, 38,
  71, 74, 76–79, 81, 84–87, 103–4, 127;
  court outcomes in, 21, 79; Democratic
  presidents and, 11; immigrant flow,
  18, 43; interest groups and, 18; organizational involvement and, 20; party
  affiliation and, 18

Basta, 118–21, 124
biases, 57; of federal courts, 21
"black letter law," 54

Board of Immigration Appeals (BIA), 14, 74–75, 78–82, 84–87, 104, 128
Bureau of Human Rights and Humanitarian Affairs (BHRHA), 77

Casa Romero, 121
Catholic Community Services, 87
Center for Constitutional Rights, 62
Central Amerian refugees, 112–15, 119, 120, 122, 125–26
certiorari, 37
Chicago Pledge of Resistance, 124
Chicago Religious Task Force on Central America (CRTFCA), 118–21
civil disobedience, 123–24
civil rights litigation, 17
civil rights movement, 85, 111, 117–18, 123
congressional policy goals, 11, 72
consciousness raising, 111
constituency, and judicial decisions, 29
consumer protection movement, 111
contextual variables, 11, 78
Corbett, Jim, 113–14, 119
country of origin, and asylum, 20
courts: legitimacy of, 4;
    lobbying of, 8; as policy makers, 58
crime rate, and court outcomes, 24

data, problems with, 18
decision making: and civil servants, 74; and economics, 11; flawed, 4; judicial, 27, 38; law school model of, 12; variables, 5
decision rules: agencies and, 12; unclear, 72
decisions, publication of, 18
deportation proceedings, 13–14, 75
diplomatic relations, and extradition requests, 41
discretion: courts and, 6–7; in decision making, 42

economic factors, and asylum-related appeals, 23
Elder, Jack, 121
El Salvador, 112–13, 122, 124

enabling statutes, conflicting, 12
entrenched organizations, 115–17, 121, 122–25, 128
environmental issues, and judicial decision making, 17
environmental policy, 37
environmental protection movement, 111
environmental variables, and judicial decision making, 16, 59
Escobedo v. United States, 37
ethnic lobby, 46–47
ethnic politics, 51, 105
exclusion, 75
external organizations, 39–40, 45; relators and, 45
extradition, 44; case law, 37, 42; cases, 38–39; federal court ruling, 36; request, 36–37; treaties, 5, 6, 36, 37, 42
Extradition Act of 1981, 44
extraneous variables: and decision making, 15; and federal court outcomes, 15

facts, and law, 4, 39
federal court appeals, 84
federal court decision making, 81–82, 104
federal court decisions, 79
federal court judges: and extradition case, 40; and organizations, 10; as political activists, 9; and political careers, 22, 42; politcal influence and, 11; region and, 17
federal courts: as apolitical, 21, 73; as policy makers, 16, 68; as political actors, 9; and political influence, 73
federal courts of appeal, 17
findings, factual and legal, 18
foreign policy goals, and administrative agencies, 15
free-rider problem, 84
fringe organizations, 65, 116–18, 121, 123, 124, 127
fundamentalist Christian movement, 111, 117

gay rights movement, 111
general model of public law, 103–4
geographic region, 41, 59, 105; court locations and, 39;

judges and, 17, 19
governmental reform movement, 111
Guatemala, 112–13, 122, 124
guilty plea, as sentencing variable, 31

habeas corpus, 37
Haitian Refugee Center, 87
holding, 18; difficulty in determining, 12
Honduras, 113
hostile countries, 13, 39, 76, 78–80, 84, 104, 112, 128
hostile country bias, 15, 17, 84–85, 87

ideology, judicial decisions and, 22
immigrants, 16, 85; flow of, 19; integrated, 22
Immigration and Nationality Act of 1952, 14, 75
Immigration and Naturalization Service (INS), 13, 76
immigration appeals, 18
immigration bureaucracy, 84, 86–87, 112
immigration laws, 112
immigration policy, 78
impartiality of judges, 4
interest groups, 38, 43–45, 58, 60, 62, 66, 73–74, 78, 104, 105, 115, 126–27; and abortion cases, 60, 66; and asylum related appeals, 19, 23; countermobilization of, 85; involvement in appeals, 79; in litigation, 5, 8, 12, 16; litigation success, 10; private, 85
international crime, 39
international extradition: and news media, 44; proceedings, 6. *See also* extradition
Irish Republican Army (IRA), 39, 45, 49–51, 105
Irish Republcan Party, 10

Jewish lobby, Palestinians and, 47
joint litigation, 86
Judeo-Christian culture, legal systems and, 3
judges: and age, 29; as decision makers, 12; and future promotion, 9; impartiality of, 4; influences on, 7; as interpreters of law, 4; and judicial

constituencies, 35; objectivity of, 4; partisan affiliation of, 5, 9, 34, 40; as policy makers, 5, 12; political pasts of, 10; and political variables, 8, 10, 28, 73; and public opinion, 35; socialization of, 3
judicial adjudication, 71
judicial constituencies, 16, 38, 58, 103–5; and decisions, 5; and, public opinion, 8
judicial decision makers, 71, 72
judicial decision making, 71, 78, 104, 105; ambiguity in, 54; analysis of, 11; facts and, 3; and ideology, 11; law school model, 3; and political affiliation, 16; political factors and, 7, 57; public opinion and, 16; regional considerations, 11; variables, 5, 16
judicial election, 34
judicial nomination, 34
judicial objectivity, 4
judicial selection, 22
judiciary, research on, 11
judiciary symbols, 4

Kaine, Thomas, 48
King, Reverend Martin Luther, Jr., 111, 116

law: agreement on, 4; as constraint, 37; uniformity of, 4
law and facts, 5, 7, 12, 42, 67, 72
law school model, of decision making, 12, 72
legal appeals, 4
legal interest groups, 116, 127
legal organizations, 116
legal services organizations, 82–84
legal standards, vagueness of, 5, 37
legitimacy, judicial, 4
libertarians, 64
litigants, 4
litigation: abortion-related, 54; and interest groups, 10, 66; and pro-abortion groups, 55, 67
litigation-related factors, in decision making, 72
litigation resources, 45, 78, 86; and individuals, 23; organizations and, 10; and

"repeat players," 23, 73
Loder, Ted, 115
Lynchehaun, James, 48

Merkdt, Stacey, 121
misrepresentation of facts, 12
moral law, 117–18
Muhlenkamp, Dianne, 121

National Association for the Advancement
    of Colored People (NAACP), 111–12
National Medical Association, 62
National Organization for Women
    (NOW), 62, 66
National Right to Life Committee, 64
natural justice, 109
natural law, 109–17, 119, 121, 123, 124,
    128; and Christian philosophers, 110
New Deal laws, and Supreme
    Court, 6
non-hostile countries, 15, 39, 80, 82, 84
non-legal variables, in extradition cases,
    38
non-political variables, influence on judi-
    cial decision making, 11
non-transitivity, 18

Operation Rescue, 65
organizational involvement, 80, 87; in
    appeals, 20, 82
organizations: and litigation resources, 23,
    73; Palestinian, 47

Palestine Liberation Organization (PLO),
    10, 39, 45, 51, 105
Palestinian organizations, 47
partisanship, and judges, 5, 9, 18, 21–22,
    38, 40, 44, 57, 60, 73, 104–5
peace movement, 111, 117
penumbras, in Bill of Rights, 55
persecution: clear probability of, 14; defi-
    nition of, 5; fear of, 13
Planned Parenthood, 62
Plaster v. United States, 37
Plato, 109
Pledge of Resistance (POR), 123–24, 127
policy goals, 72, 116
policy makers, 117

policy making: and constituency prefer-
    ences, 16; courts and, 57
political actors, 43; federal courts as, 9,
    43
political asylum, 13, 67, 74, 113; mecha-
    nisms for, 75
political environment, 8, 21
political factors, 7, 8, 42, 57, 63, 104, 105
political offense exception, to extradition,
    39, 41, 42, 45, 49
political variables, 103; abortion cases
    and, 57, 66; appeals and, 11; and a-
    sylum-related appeals, 11; judicial
    decisions and, 38; in public law, 8; and
    state courts, 28
positive law, 109–19, 121, 123–25, 128
precedent, 72; unreliability of, 12
privacy interests, of women, 55
privacy right, 55
private foundations, 85, 117
pro-abortion movement, 57–59, 61–62,
    63, 64, 65–66, 67, 68, 105
Proyecto Libertad, 126
public interest groups, 73, 85–87; in
    asylum-related appeals, 85; legal, 85
public law: general theory of, 7, 103;
    research contradictions in, 7
public opinion, 16; judges and, 22; as
    political variable, 16

Quinn v. Robinson, 49

race, and asylum, 24
rape, 24–36; reform of legislation, 24–27
rape sentencing, 27–36; criminal justice
    variables, 29–30; data, 30–32; political
    variables, 28–29
"reasonable man" determination, 4
Re Extradition of Prushinowski, 37
refuge, 39
Refugee Act of 1980, 13, 15, 74, 76–77,
    85
refugee and asylum policy, 79, 84, 128
refugees, 13, 120, 126; and asylees, 74,
    85, 104; defined, 15, 74; policy relating
    to, 37; political, 49
region, 53, 63; as contextual variable, 16,
    67; and court outcomes, 67

regulations, 71
relators, 39, 43–44, 51; definition of, 10, 45; and external organizations, 40
Religious Coalition for Abortion Rights, 62
religious organizations, 85, 117, 120–24; and abortion, 67
"repeat players," 23, 73, 78, 86
request for asylum, 14
research, on judiciary, 11
reversals, 4
right reason, as law, 110
right to privacy, 54
Roe v. Wade, 53, 55–57, 59, 63–66, 68
rule making, 72

sanctuary, 112, 119
sanctuary movement, 111, 113–15, 118–26, 128
sentencing decisions: discretion in, 29; district court, 30; policy objectives and, 27; variables in, 29
sexism, 25
sex offenses. *See* rape; rape sentencing
social movements, 109, 111, 115–18, 126–28
social support, judicial opinions and, 22
social welfare interest groups, 116
standing, 68
state abortion policy, 68
state court judges: and public opinion, 29; selection of, 28. *See also* judges

state crime, 39
state interests, 85
state law, versus federal law, 19, 59
statutes, vagueness of, 5, 12
Supreme Court, and support of civil liberties, 6

tax revolt movement of 1977–80, 111
Thomas Aquinas, Saint, 110
Tucson Ecumenical Council, 119
"Tucson trial," 121, 124

underground railroad, 120
unemployment rate, 80, 82; and asylum, 18, 19, 79; and immigration policy, 17, 79
United States Catholic Conference, 125
United Way, 125

variables, in court outcomes, 32
viability, of fetal life, 56

Webster v. Reproductive Health Services, 65
withholding of application, 14
withholding of deportation, 13–14, 67, 74–75, 112, 126
women: and abortion decisions, 58; as judicial constituency, 30, 60
Women Abused by Abortion, 65
Women's Equity Action League (WEAL), 126
women's groups, 55; state judges and, 32
women's movement, 111, 126

ABOUT THE AUTHOR

BARBARA M. YARNOLD is Assistant Professor in the Department of Public Administration at Florida International University and an attorney. She is the editor of *The Role of Religious Organizations in Social Movements* (Praeger, 1991) and the author of *International Fugitives: A New Role for the International Court of Justice* (Praeger, 1991), *Refugees Without Refuge* (1990), and numerous articles on public law.